2ND EDITION

EXTRAORDINARY BLACK MISSOURIANS

PIONEERS, LEADERS, PERFORMERS, ATHLETES, AND OTHER NOTABLES
WHO'VE MADE HISTORY

Toussaint L'Ouverture

Toussaint L'Ouverture

1743–1803

MISSOURI'S UNSUNG HERO

Toussaint L'Ouverture led a 1791 revolt against the French and set in motion events that culminated in the Haitian Revolution and independence. The loss of Haiti left Napoleon desperate, and he squelched his plans for a French empire in North America and went in search of ways to raise money. The Louisiana Territory became expendable, facilitating the Louisiana Purchase.

To our children and to our grandchildren:

John III, Anastasia, Chloi, Haley, Curtis Jr.,

Clayton, Caleb, Ezana, and Isabella.

Reedy Press
PO Box 5131
St. Louis, MO 63139, USA
www.reedypress.com

No part of this publication may be reproduced or transmitted in any form or
by any means, electronic or mechanical, including photocopy, recording, or
any information storage and retrieval system, without permission in writing
from the publisher.

Permissions may be sought directly from Reedy Press at the above mailing
address or via our website at www.reedypress.com.

Library of Congress Control Number: 2020950003

ISBN: 9781681063027

Cover design by Eric Marquard
Cover images: *Leon Jordan, courtesy of Mercantile Library at UMSL; Frankie
Freeman, courtesy of Getty Images; Chuck Berry, public domain; Lou Brock, courtesy
of Mercantile Library at UMSL; Charles Henry Turner, courtesy of St. Louis Public
Schools; Josephine Baker, courtesy of Getty Images; George Washington, courtesy of
Oregon Historical Society; Maxine Waters, courtesy of Maxine Waters*
Interior design by Renee Duenow

Printed in the United States of America
21 22 23 24 25   5 4 3 2 1

ontents

Performers, Athletes, and Other Notables

Acknowledgments

A book such as this could not have been done without the assistance from a number of individuals and institutions, and we would like to acknowledge them. A special thanks goes to Charles Brown and the Mercantile Library at the University of Missouri–St. Louis (UMSL): without their support this book would not have been possible. Charles was always available when called upon and never hesitated in responding to requests throughout the project. A special thanks also goes to Reedy Press for their support throughout the development of the book.

Other individuals are: Janet Robinson Bosley, Arnold Parks, Gary Kremer, Erica Neal, Barbara Gill, Henry Givens Jr., Donald Suggs, Eric Rome, Lois Conley, Charles Cross, Maxine Waters, Angela DaSilva, DeBorah Ahmed, Emanuel Cleaver, Philip White, Arzelia Gates, Kenneth Webb, Frances Bullitt Reed, George Draper, Ida Early, Gerald Early, Ron Himes, Carol Porter, Olly Wilson Jr., John Abram, Barbara Washington, Debra Foster Greene, Raymond Doswell, James Brown, Rob Kravitz, Sharon Doland, and Arnold Parks.

The institutions are Library of Congress; Department of the Interior Bureau of Pensions; National Archives; Henderson House Museum, Tumwater, Washington; Minnesota Historical Society; Central Baptist Church; Oregon Historical Society;

Society of California Pioneers; Washington University in St. Louis Archives; Griot Museum; City of St. Louis; St. Louis Public Schools; State Historical Society of Missouri; Western Historical Manuscript Collection at the University of Missouri–St. Louis; Julia Davis Branch of the St. Louis Public Library; Picture Collection at Inman E. Page Library, Lincoln University; Annie Malone Children and Family Service Center; State of Missouri; US Supreme Court; Saint Louis University Archives; Baseball Hall of Fame Library, Cooperstown, New York; Derrty Entertainment; and Negro Leagues Baseball Museum in Kansas City.

The writers would be remiss if they did not recognize Betty Wheeler, Earl Wilson Jr., John Bass, Billye Crumpton, Doris Wesley, Julia Davis, Jerome Williams Sr., Frankie Freeman, Patricia McKissack and Sister Mary Antona Ebo, who provided the writers with valuable information and pictures used in the book prior to their deaths.

John A. Wright Sr.,
Sylvia A. Wright,
and
John A. Wright Jr.

$\mathcal{I}$ntroduction

$\mathcal{A}$frican Americans have been a part of Missouri for over 293 years. They were first brought to the Missouri Territory from Haiti by the French in 1720, as enslaved individuals to work in the lead mines in the Mine La Motte area. When one considers that for almost half of that 293 years the overwhelming majority of African Americans in the state were enslaved and for another 100 years they were treated as second-class citizens, it is a marvel that out of such a cruel beginning African Americans have played a major role in shaping the history and culture of the state and nation.

The dictionary defines *extraordinary* as beyond the ordinary, very unusual and exceptional. Individuals are not born with these traits but develop them over time through their life experiences. This book is filled with extraordinary individuals who have spent most or part of their lives in Missouri and who saw wrong and worked to right it, regardless of personal cost. The book contains individuals who had dreams and ideas and chose to pursue them when others around them had little or no belief in them. And the book features individuals who spent unending hours and days developing their God-given talents. Many became superstars in the arts, sports, science, literature, civil rights, military, entertainment, law, education, and business, while others were just ordinary people whose extraordinary determination enabled them to change the course of history. Almost all of the individuals in the book had to overcome formidable obstacles and endure painful experiences with little to sustain them but their own willpower, faith, determination, and courage.

We realize the individuals in this book constitute only a small fraction of the countless number of African Americans who have added to the growth and development of Missouri and America. We know that there are a number of individuals who will never be recognized because their stories have never been told and their heroic deeds have been lost over time. This book, however, features individuals from diverse backgrounds and walks of life from across the state with extraordinary stories that are representative of the countless other stories waiting to be told and written.

We hope that *Extraordinary Black Missourians* will serve as an inspiration and encouragement to those whose dreams are moving along or in the struggling stage, on hold, or waiting to be developed. The stories of the individuals in this book stand as testimonials for what can be done when there is determination and faith in oneself. It is our desire that this book will also serve as a source of reference for those seeking information on the contributions of African Americans to the state and nation, and it will inspire in them a desire to expand and broaden their knowledge of African Americans. If this occurs our effort as writers will be well rewarded.

John A. Wright Sr.,
Sylvia A. Wright,
and
John A. Wright Jr.

2ND EDITION

EXTRAORDINARY
BLACK MISSOURIANS

PIONEERS, LEADERS, PERFORMERS, ATHLETES, AND OTHER NOTABLES
WHO'VE MADE HISTORY

JOHN A. WRIGHT SR., SYLVIA A. WRIGHT,
& JOHN A. WRIGHT JR.

"Lose not courage, lose not
faith, go forward."
—*Marcus Garvey*

Pioneers

"If there is no struggle, there is
no progress."
—*Frederick Douglass*

Archer Alexander

1810–1879

MODEL FOR FREEDMEN'S MONUMENT

In Lincoln Park in Washington, D.C., a bronze monument depicts President Abraham Lincoln reaching out to a crouching figure who is working to free himself from chains. Archer Alexander, formerly enslaved, is the figure immortalized in this monument, which also is known as the Emancipation Memorial or the Freedmen's Memorial.

Alexander was born into enslavement on a Virginia plantation around 1813. When he was in his teens he was separated from his mother and sent to Missouri, where he was hired out to local brickyards in St. Louis. While in St. Louis, he met and married an enslaved woman named Louisa, and they had several children.

In 1863, Alexander put his life in danger by warning Union troops that a pro-slavery party had cut the timbers of a certain bridge so that it would collapse while carrying a detachment of Union troops. The detachment was saved. Alexander was suspected as the informant and arrested by a pro-slavery committee. He escaped, and was later hired by William Greenleaf Eliot, a minister, abolitionist, and the founder of Washington University in St. Louis. Eliot hid Alexander from slave catchers until the passage of the Emancipation Proclamation.

Alexander, Louisa, and some of their children were reunited for only a short time. In 1866, his wife died of a mysterious disease. Alexander later remarried and lived near Eliot. In 1876, Thomas Ball designed and sculpted the Emancipation Memorial

under the direction of Eliot, who hired Alexander to pose for the statue. Alexander is said to have seen a picture of the completed monument prior to his death on December 8, 1879.

James Beckwourth
1798–1866
CROW CHIEF AND FUR TRADER

No group of men contributed more to the development of the West than the explorers who opened up the land west of the Appalachian Mountains. While James P. Beckwourth's contemporaries Kit Carson and Daniel Boone are household names, Beckwourth's has been deleted from memory and his story is no longer told in many of our history books. Yet Beckwourth's life as a mountain man was just as vibrant and filled with adventure as those of his white peers.

Beckwourth was born in Fredericksburg, Virginia, on April 6, 1798, the third of thirteen children. His father, Ezra, a white officer in the Revolutionary War, moved his family to St. Louis County in 1810 to escape widespread resentment of his marriage to an enslaved Black woman who had worked as a servant in his household.

Around 1817, Beckwourth began a five-year apprenticeship at John Sutton and George Casner's blacksmith shop in St. Louis. Beckwourth, said to tire quickly of Casner's attempts to control his life, went to work at his father's trading post and in the lead mines near Galena, Illinois. In 1824, Beckwourth joined General William Ashley's fur trapping expedition, which took him up the Mississippi River and into the Rocky Mountains.

On that expedition, Beckwourth was adopted by the Crow Indians when an old squaw insisted he was her long-lost son. He quickly rose in the ranks of tribal leadership. Renamed "Morning

Star," Beckwourth married the chief's daughter and led the Crow braves on raids against the Blackfeet, their sworn enemies. Eventually he was chosen to assume the role of chief.

After a few years, Beckwourth left the Crow tribe to resume his wandering. He served with the Missouri volunteers as an army scout during the Third Seminole War in Florida, and he assisted General Philip Kearny during California's revolt against Mexico. His biggest contribution to Kearny was obtaining a treaty with the Apaches so that the general could send couriers between Fort Leavenworth and General Sterling Price in Santa Fe.

In April 1850, Beckwourth made a discovery that should have secured him a place in Western history forever. He found an important passageway through the Sierra Nevada range that now bears his name. He personally guided the first seventeen wagons filled with adventurers stricken with "gold fever" through the pass.

Legend has it that Beckwourth was invited by the Crow to again lead the tribe, and when he refused he was poisoned and his body was placed in their burial grounds. However, it is believed Beckwourth died in 1866 of food poisoning in the Plains on his way to a Crow village.

William Wells Brown

1814–1884

When studying the life of William Wells Brown one is amazed by the various roles he played—enslaved man, fugitive, steamboat worker, anti-slavery activist, orator, essayist, newspaperman, playwright, historian, sociologist, doctor, and temperance reformer. The fact that he did not learn to read or write until he was in his early twenties is even more striking.

This famous American was born in 1814 in Lexington, Kentucky, one of seven children belonging to an enslaved woman by the name of Elizabeth. His father, George W. Higgins, was a close friend of Dr. John Young, the white owner of the plantation on which Brown was born. Until he was twenty years old, Brown was known simply as William. His name was taken away from him when the Youngs adopted an infant nephew with the same name. Since William had a light complexion, the Youngs renamed him Sanford to prevent confusion.

In 1827, Dr. Young moved to St. Louis, taking William and his mother along. In St. Louis, Elizabeth and all of her children, except William, were sold to different people. Dr. Young hired William out to at least ten different employers. One was Elijah P. Lovejoy, whom William credits with the little learning he received during slavery. Another employer was James Walker, a slave dealer. William was responsible for preparing enslaved persons for sale.

His last employer was Enoch Price, a merchant and steamboat owner from whom he escaped. Brown went on to assist those escaping enslavement and lectured on the evils of slavery in New England and Great Britain. He traveled more than 25,000 miles and addressed more than 1,000 public meetings. He met Victor Hugo and was made an honorary member of the London Club, to which Charles Dickens belonged. And in 1852 William was one of the founders of a London newspaper, the *Anti-Slavery Advocate*.

After the Civil War, Brown continued to work for peace and temperance but devoted most of his energies to defend African Americans against oppressors and to secure for them the rights guaranteed in the US Constitution. Although this took up a great deal of his time, he practiced medicine, and by 1864 he was actively treating patients and used the title "Mom and Dad" after his name.

Brown is considered the first African American historian, as well as novelist and playwright. His literary career began in 1847 with the publication of his *Narrative of William W. Brown, a Fugitive Slave, Written by Himself*, which provided readers with a graphic picture of slavery in St. Louis. Brown died on November 6, 1884, from an ailment associated with a tumor of the bladder.

$\mathcal{B}$lanche Kelso Bruce

ca. 1841–1898

US SENATOR

*T*he youngest of eleven children, Blanche Kelso Bruce was born enslaved in Prince Edward County, Virginia, on March 1, 1841, to Pettis Perkinson, a white Virginia plantation owner, and Polly Bruce, an enslaved house worker on Perkinson's estate. Perkinson ensured Bruce an education by having Bruce's half brother tutor him after school. After relocating to Chariton County, Missouri, and Mississippi before returning back to Virginia, Bruce was legally freed by his father.

Newly freed at the onset of the Civil War, Bruce moved to Lawrence, Kansas, and established the state's first school for African Americans. By the end of the war, Bruce was in Hannibal, Missouri, and opened another school for African Americans, again a first for this state. His accomplishments aside, Bruce was profoundly disappointed after being rejected by the Union Army. In 1866, he entered Oberlin College in Ohio but left before obtaining a degree, due to financial constraints. Again, Bruce returned to Missouri and worked as a steamboat porter.

In 1869, Bruce moved to Mississippi and became a prosperous landowner and served as sheriff and tax collector of Bolivar County and a member of the Mississippi Levee Board. In 1874, the Mississippi Legislature elected Bruce to the US Senate, where he became the first African American to serve a full term and the first to preside over a Senate session. During his term he advocated fair treatment for African Americans and Indians, and

he opposed a policy to exclude Chinese immigrants, all for the betterment of race relations.

After the Reconstruction government ended in the South, Bruce lost his political base and ended his time in the Senate. He remained in Washington, D.C. In 1880 at the Republican National Convention, Bruce was nominated for vice president, becoming the first African American to receive a nomination by a major party. Bruce was appointed register of the Treasury (1895–1898), where his signature appeared on US currency. Bruce also served as recorder of deeds in the District of Columbia (1889–1893) and trustee of Howard University, while he edited a local newspaper.

Bruce died on March 17, 1898, in Washington, D.C.

George Washington Bush

ca. 1790–1863
PIONEER

George Washington Bush was a leader of the first group of American citizens to settle north of the Columbia River in what is now the state of Washington. Bush was born a free man around 1790, the son of servants for a wealthy Quaker family in Pennsylvania. His father was African American and his mother was Irish American. Educated in the Quaker tradition, Bush served in the US Army before embarking on a career as a fur trapper and explorer for the Hudson's Bay Company, the St. Louis–based Robidoux Company, and the Oregon Territory.

Bush eventually settled in Clay County, Missouri, and earned a good livelihood farming and raising cattle. He married Isabella James, a German American, and started a family. With the Civil War looming and an increasing climate of bigotry against African Americans, Bush soon headed west with his wife and their six children.

Five white families—friends and neighbors of the Bushes— joined them on their journey. The families later fell in with a larger wagon train and left Missouri in May 1844. Bush and longtime friend Michael Simmons led the train, and Bush's experience as a fur trapper proved invaluable. Bush was reportedly one of the more wealthy pioneers to take the Oregon Trail, with rumors of a false floor in his Conestoga wagon that concealed a layer of silver dollars.

When the wagon train reached the Columbia River, the Bushes found the Oregon Territory provisional government had enacted legislation similar to laws in Missouri that barred settlement of African Americans. As a show of solidarity, the group decided to move on to a region not controlled by such legislation. The following year, they became the first Americans to settle in the Puget Sound region. Bush started a farm near present-day Olympia, Washington, and his family was known for their generosity to new arrivals and for their friendship with Native Americans.

When Oregon Territory law absorbed the region, it denied African Americans the right to own land. In 1854, Bush's friends—who were territorial legislators—voted unanimously for a resolution urging Congress to pass a special act confirming Bush's title to his land. Congress did so a year later.

Celia

1836–1855
ENSLAVED GIRL

The horrors of slavery are exemplified by the story of Celia. In 1850, fourteen-year-old Celia was living with her enslaved parents in Audrain Country, Missouri, when she was purchased by Robert Newsom, a Callaway County farmer. Newsom, a seventy-year-old grandfather and widower, began to have carnal relations with Celia immediately after purchasing her. Celia lived in a cabin about sixty steps from his home with her two children, each fathered by Newsom.

A young enslaved African American man named George lived nearby, and Celia developed strong feelings for him. Over time, George came to consider Celia as his wife, and he bitterly resented Newsom's periodic intrusions. George told Celia that if she did not stop acquiescing to the old man, he would have nothing to do with her.

On the night of June 23, 1855, despite Celia's repeated warnings to stay away, Newsom visited her cabin. Earlier, Celia had told Newsom that she "would hurt him if he did not quit forcing relations with her while she was sick." Celia had been pregnant for several months with another of Newsom's children. This particular evening, when Newsom advanced toward her, she struck him on the head with a stick and killed him. Celia then burned his body in the fireplace of her cabin, and carried out the ashes the next morning.

A search of the ashes by local officials revealed buttons and bits of bone. An inquest was held, and Celia was jailed until her

WINSLOW HOMER PRINT *AT THE CABIN DOOR*, 1865

trial in October. Celia was found guilty and sentenced to hang on November 16, 1855. Her attorneys immediately asked for a stay while they appealed to the Missouri Supreme Court. Soon after, the young woman delivered a stillborn child. To prevent her execution before a court decision was handed down, Celia was assisted in escaping from the jail. After the date of her scheduled execution passed, she was caught and returned to jail.

The Supreme Court appeal was denied, and Celia was hanged on December 21, 1855, in Fulton, Missouri. Many felt the court's decision was a foregone conclusion, since three of the judges had ruled in the Dred Scott case. However, it is safe to assume that Celia's acquittal was never possible because that would have undermined the assumption of complete control of white male ownership over their property.

$\mathcal{A}$lvin Coffey

1822–1902
PIONEER

$\mathcal{A}$lvin Aaron Coffey, the only African American inducted into the California Society of Pioneers, was born into enslavement on July 14, 1822, in Mason County, Kentucky. He was the son of Lewis Larkin Coffey and Nellie Cook Coffey. In 1843, Coffey was sold by Margaret Cooke to Henry H. Duvall, who took him to Missouri. Duval later sold Coffey to William Basset for six hundred dollars. On April 2, 1849, Basset left St. Louis with Coffey, headed for St. Joseph, Missouri, to join a wagon train being assembled to travel to California. Coffey was forced to leave behind his wife, who was pregnant with their third child, and their two other children.

The wagon train pulled out of St. Joseph on May 2, 1849, and arrived in Redding Springs, California, on October 13, 1849. Coffey immediately went to work searching for gold for himself and Basset, who had been ill during the entire trip. After two years, Basset decided to return to Missouri.

Coffey had earned five thousand dollars for his owner and seven hundred dollars for himself from mining and by washing clothes for other miners. Once in Missouri, Basset defrauded Coffey of his earnings and sold him for one thousand dollars to the Tindall family, who already owned Coffey's wife and children. Coffey persuaded the Tindalls to allow him to return to the California gold fields to earn money to purchase himself and his family. Coffey traveled back to California, and by 1856

he earned enough to purchase his own freedom. A year later, he had earned an additional seven thousand dollars to purchase freedom for the rest of his family.

Coffey returned to Missouri in 1857 to reunite with his wife and three sons and then took them to California. The younger children were sent to Canada with their grandmother until the Coffeys could get established. The family settled in Shasta County, California, on a small plot of land. When the children returned from Canada, they attended a school for African Americans and Native Americans in Shasta County that Coffey had helped found in 1858. During the Modoc Indian War, Coffey provided horses for the US Army and provided his services as a teamster. Coffey also earned income by operating a laundry and raising turkeys.

Coffey and his descendants went on to prosper throughout the state. He died on October 28, 1902. His fellow members of the Society of California Pioneers members attended the funeral.

$\mathcal{M}$oses Dickson

1824–1901
A Moses Who Fought to Liberate His People

One night in 1846, thirteen men met in a house on the southeast corner of Green and Seventh streets in St. Louis to plot a revolution. Led by the Reverend Moses Dickson, a Cincinnati native and free Black man who observed the evils of slavery during a tour of the South in the early 1840s, the men founded a group known as the Knights of Liberty. The Knights sought to end slavery through armed engagement.

Originally, the group had planned to send 150,000 or more armed men into Atlanta, Georgia, but Dickson reconsidered this approach as the Knights prepared to move forward in the summer of 1857. He sensed the coming of the Civil War over the question of slavery, and decided it would be better to have white men involved in the anti-slavery effort. With Dickson's decision, the Knights' method of operation switched from outright rebellion to underground resistance. The Knights teamed with the Union forces during the war and caused numerous fatalities.

After the war, Dickson returned to Missouri, where he was ordained as a minister in the African Methodist Episcopal Church. He was among the founders of Lincoln Institute in Jefferson City (now Lincoln University), and he petitioned the Missouri Legislature to foster the growth of African American schools by approving a legal doctrine of "separate but equal." Together with political leader and fellow Missourian James Milton Turner,

Dickson fought to give African Americans the vote in Missouri. A prominent St. Louis citizen and president of the Refugee Relief Board, Dickson assisted in finding new homes for approximately 16,000 Southern refugees and former slaves in 1878. Fourteen years later, to bring to light the problem of violent crimes against Black citizens, he campaigned across Missouri with other well-known Black leaders.

The Reverend Dickson died in his home at 2651 Pine Street in St. Louis on November 28, 1901. His funeral was reported to be one of the most elaborate St. Louisans had ever seen.

$\mathcal{J}$ean Baptiste Point DuSable

1745–1818
THE FIRST CITIZEN OF CHICAGO

$\mathcal{J}$ean Baptiste Point DuSable, the founder of Chicago, is buried in an unmarked grave in the old section of Borromeo Cemetery in St. Charles, Missouri. Records show he was born in St. Mare, Haiti, in 1745, to a French mariner father and an African-born enslaved mother. After his mother's death, his father sent him to Paris to be educated. Later, he worked as a seaman on his father's ship.

At the age of twenty, DuSable was shipwrecked and injured near the coast of New Orleans. Fearful that he might be enslaved, he persuaded French Jesuits to hide him until he was well enough to travel. After leaving New Orleans, he headed up the Mississippi River to St. Louis, where he developed a thriving trading business with a Frenchman named Jacques Clamorgan, an individual believed to be of African descent.

In the mid-1770s, DuSable left St. Louis for Peoria, Illinois, where he bought some land and developed contacts among the Indians. After learning several Indian dialects, in 1779 he headed for the area now known as Chicago, where he began a fur-trading business. Though DuSable made a living trading furs he was also a miller, cooper, and farmer. DuSable lived for sixteen years on the north bank of the Chicago River, where he fell in love with a Potawatomi woman named Catherine. DuSable was Catholic but found it difficult to follow his religion in the wilderness. In 1788, he traveled to Cahokia with his wife to have a priest confirm his

marriage in a religious ceremony. In 1790, he traveled to St. Louis for the marriage of his daughter at the old St. Louis Cathedral, and he returned again in 1799 for the baptism of her first child.

In 1800, DuSable abruptly sold his real estate holdings and personal property. The impressive contents of his nine buildings included a French walnut cabinet with glass doors, feather beds, copper kettles, carpentry tools, and a host of farm instruments. The DuSables then moved in with their daughter in St. Charles.

As his life drew to a close, DuSable worried about the future. He did not want to become a public charge, dependent on the community, and he wanted to be buried in a Catholic cemetery. The priest of St. Charles Borromeo Church recorded DuSable's death on August 28, 1818.

Robert Hickman

1831–1900

ABOLITIONIST

*B*orn into slavery in Boone County, Missouri, in 1831, as a young man Robert Hickman worked as a rail-splitter. His owner allowed Hickman to read and write, which enabled him to become a preacher for the people held in captivity in the area. As a preacher, he quickly earned the trust of those he would later lead to freedom.

One evening in 1863, Hickman led a group of enslaved persons to their freedom aboard a crude raft that they had constructed. The fugitives were almost to Jefferson City before a passing steamboat discovered them adrift. They were rescued and towed upriver, and they arrived in St. Paul, Minnesota, on May 5, 1863.

The newcomers, who referred to themselves as "pilgrims," quickly found work as laborers and teamsters. Hickman's priority was to find a place of worship for the group. After worshipping in homes, eventually they found a room to rent in a downtown concert hall. In January 1864, Hickman and the pilgrims received mission status from the First Baptist Church of St. Paul, where they officially organized Pilgrim Baptist Church, the first African American church in the city.

Despite Hickman's prominent role in getting the settlers to Minnesota and the founding of Pilgrim Baptist Church, he

was not licensed to preach there. Between 1866 and 1877, two white ministers, William Norris and Andrew Torbert, led Pilgrim Baptist. Hickman eventually became licensed to preach in 1878 and guided the church until his retirement in 1886. He died on February 6, 1900, in St. Paul.

Elizabeth Keckley

1818–1907

Author, Dressmaker, Teacher, and Confidante

lizabeth Hobbs Keckley, a former enslaved woman, was Mary Todd Lincoln's choice for a dressmaker when the First Lady came to the White House. Keckley's skill, tact, and trustworthiness endeared her to Mrs. Lincoln, and Keckley became her personal maid, travel companion, nurse, and confidante.

Keckley shared all the joys and sorrows of the Lincoln family and helped to nurse their son Willie in his fatal illness. She also aided in washing and preparing the boy's body for burial. She comforted Mrs. Lincoln when the loss of Willie brought her to the edge of a breakdown, and Keckley was by her side again three years later after the president was assassinated.

The first Black woman to enter the White House the day after Lincoln's inauguration, Keckley was born in Dinwiddie County, Virginia, in 1818 to George and Agnes Hobbs, enslaved parents on different plantations. In her teens, Keckley was taken to St. Louis by her owner, Anne Burwell Garland, and Garland's husband.

Keckley soon became known for her skill as a seamstress and dressmaker. Her earnings were used to help support the Garland family, who recognized Keckley's potential and gave her permission to move about the city. She became an active member of First African Baptist Church, where, under the guise of a sewing class, she taught children to read and write and also assisted John

Berry Meachum in giving aid to Blacks.

Determined to purchase her freedom, Keckley secured a loan of twelve hundred dollars and then worked for five years to pay off her debt while supporting an alcoholic husband. In the spring of 1860, she boarded a train to Washington, D.C., where Keckley developed a thriving sewing business, attracting rich and famous customers. She was introduced to Mrs. Lincoln, who hired her to make her inaugural gown. At this point Keckley began a new life as a woman of political influence. Over time, she was able to gently inform Mrs. Lincoln of the horrors of slavery, and Mrs. Lincoln in turn told the president.

In the spring of 1868, Keckley published her book, *Behind the Scenes; Or, Thirty Years a Slave, and Four Years in the White House*. The book provided insight into the Lincoln presidency, and Keckley hoped it would earn money that could assist Mrs. Lincoln after the president's assassination. However, the book had a different effect—because Keckley revealed personal communication between Mrs. Lincoln and herself, the book turned the Lincoln family against her. Keckley died of a paralytic stroke on May 26, 1907, in Washington, D.C.

John Berry Meachum

1789–1854

MINISTER, ABOLITIONIST, BUSINESSMAN, CARPENTER, CABINETMAKER, AND EDUCATION PIONEER

The Reverend John Berry Meachum was born into slavery in Virginia on May 3, 1789, the son of Thomas and Patsy Granger. The boy and his family soon were separated when he and his mother were taken to North Carolina and later to Kentucky.

By saving money he earned laboring in a saltpeter cave in Kentucky, as a young man he was able to purchase his freedom and that of his father. He then took the name of his former owner, Meachum, and went in search of his mother. Meachum learned that his mother, his wife, and his children all had been taken to Missouri Territory. He paid two of the three dollars he had on him to cross the Mississippi River and arrived in St. Louis in 1815.

In 1825, Meachum became an ordained minister and founded the First African Baptist Church on Third and Almond streets, the first church established for African Americans in St. Louis. When the church was founded, it had 220 members—200 were slaves who attended with permission from their owners. Meachum served as pastor for over thirty-eight years.

Shortly after the church was constructed, Meachum and John Mason Peck, his former pastor and a white friend, opened a day school under the guise of a Sunday school in the windowless

basement of the church. This was in direct defiance of a law issued by the St. Louis Board of Trustees, and violation of the law was punishable by twenty lashes, imprisonment, or fines.

In 1835, Meachum built a steamboat and equipped it with a library. His water vessel became a temperance boat that brought supplies to other boats up and down the Mississippi River. This venture proved to be very profitable for Meachum. With his earnings, he bought formerly enslaved Blacks, taught them a trade, and freed them after they repaid their purchase price. According to Baptist legend, during the 1840s and 1850s, in defiance of Missouri law, Meachum took children to his boat—a floating school—in the middle of the river, which was under federal jurisdiction, to be educated.

Meachum became one of the architects for the St. Louis fugitive Underground Railroad and one of the founders of the National Negro Convention, a nineteenth-century version of the National Association for the Advancement of Colored People (NAACP).

Immediately after announcing his text on Sunday morning, February 19, 1854, Meachum fell dead standing in the pulpit. He was laid to rest in the Baptist burial grounds of Bellefontaine Cemetery.

Dred Scott

1795–1858

THE SLAVE WHOSE CASE MOVED A COUNTRY

On July 1, 1847, a document was delivered into the hands of a Justice of the Peace in St. Louis. The petitioner was Dred Scott, who had no idea that his case would be one of the catalysts that would plunge a nation into a civil war. Scott was merely another enslaved individual seeking to free his family.

Dred Scott, known as Sam, was born in 1795 in Southampton, Virginia, the property of the Blow family. The family moved with Sam to St. Louis in 1830. Peter Blow, his owner, died two years later and left Sam to his daughter, who sold him to Dr. John Emerson, a surgeon in the US Army, for five hundred dollars.

In 1834, Emerson took Scott from St. Louis to Rock Island, Illinois, and later to Wisconsin Territory. Both locations prohibited slavery, according to the Missouri Compromise. While traveling abroad, Emerson bought an enslaved girl named Harriet Robinson, and in 1836, Sam and Harriet were married in a legal ceremony. The Scotts had two children, Eliza and Lizzie. Eliza died early in her teens. Lizzie lived in St. Louis until 1881.

Emerson died in 1842, shortly after returning to St. Louis. The Scotts then were entrusted to Emerson's widow, Irene Emerson. On April 6, 1846, the Scotts sued their mistress for their freedom. The Scotts' position was that their long residence on free soil in Illinois and Minnesota (which was a part of the Wisconsin Territory at the time) made them free.

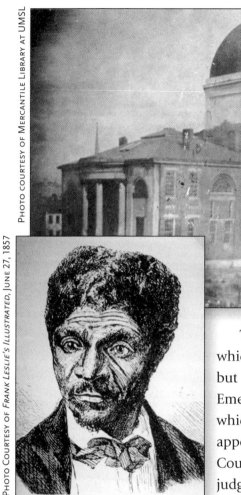

The Scotts lost at the trial, which began on June 30, 1847, but they won on appeal. Irene Emerson moved for a new trial, which was denied. In 1852, she appealed to the Missouri Supreme Court, which reversed the judgment of the lower court—and returned the Scotts to slavery.

The Scotts again filed suit in 1846. They lost their motion for a new trial. They next appealed to the United States Supreme Court, which, after argument, dismissed their case on March 6, 1851. The court declared that a slave was not a citizen and had no right to sue. The ruling caused violent political controversy and indirectly contributed to the beginning of the Civil War.

Soon after the trial, ownership of Dred Scott was transferred to Taylor Blow, the son of Peter Blow, the original owner. Taylor Blow set him free. Scott died two years later of tuberculosis.

Charlton H. Tandy

1836–1919

The Man Who Brought an End to St. Louis's Jim Crow Streetcar System

Charlton H. Tandy was born on December 16, 1836, in Lexington, Kentucky, as a free citizen. In 1857, he moved to St. Louis seeking better opportunities. When the Civil War began, Tandy was hired as a post messenger at Jefferson Barracks. Later, when Confederate soldiers were invading Missouri, Tandy was one of the first to answer the Union's call for volunteers. He enlisted in Company B of the state militia as a commissioned private and was later appointed captain of "Tandy's Saint Louis Guard," a state militia composed of Black volunteers that he had recruited. He held this position until the end of the war.

In 1867, when public transportation companies did not follow an order by the St. Louis Circuit Court to allow Blacks to ride inside their horse-drawn cars, Tandy mounted an effective protest. He stood on street corners and forced the drivers to halt by grabbing the reins and holding the horses until both Blacks and whites were allowed to ride.

In 1875, Tandy took up another battle. When the St. Louis Board of Education wanted to transfer Black students to a school located in the slums, he rallied Black leaders and parents and prevented the action. He played a major role in getting jobs for Black teachers and principals in the St. Louis Public Schools. Tandy also ended some of the discriminatory practices used against Black educators.

IN THE

Supreme Court of Missouri

DIVISION No. 1.

OCTOBER TERM, 1902.

CHARLTON H. TANDY,
(Plaintiff) Respondent,

vs.

No. 10,746.

ST. LOUIS TRANSIT COMPANY,
(Defendant) Appellant.

APPEAL FROM THE CIRCUIT COURT OF THE CITY OF ST. LOUIS, COURT ROOM NO. 5, HON. D. D. FISHER, JUDGE.

Statement and Brief for Appellant.

STATEMENT.

The petition in this case was filed in the Circuit Court on October 27, 1900, and was in substance as follows:

That on or about the 10th day of August, 1900, Annie E. Tandy, lawful wife of the plaintiff, was a passenger on a Page Avenue car owned and operated by the defendant corporation. That "while she was in the act of alighting from said car, after it had stopped on the west side of Walton avenue, at its intersection

When thousands of penniless African Americans passed through St. Louis, fleeing the South on their way to Kansas in the Exodus of 1879, Tandy organized a relief organization to aid the refugees.

Due to his support and work for the Republican Party, Tandy received a number of appointments: messenger in the US Customs Office; special agent in the Interior Department in Land Offices in New Mexico and Oklahoma; and vice president of the State League. In 1894, he was admitted to the bar and practiced in the district and supreme courts of the Oklahoma Territory.

Tandy's last days were spent as a representative of the 10th Ward in St. Louis. He died on September 11, 1919, in his home at 1224 Bayard Avenue. Though Tandy did not live to see his dream of full equality for African Americans fulfilled, his contributions to that goal were numerous—and most effective.

$\mathcal{J}$ames Milton Turner

1840–1915
DIPLOMAT, EDUCATOR, AND DEFENDER OF RIGHTS

$\mathcal{J}$ames Milton Turner refused to accept the status of inferiority. In a brief twenty-five years, he rose from enslavement to freedom and statewide prominence. By the age of thirty-one, he had been appointed minister resident and consul general of Liberia, West Africa. He was the first Missourian to receive a US diplomatic post.

Turner was born into slavery in St. Louis County on May 16, 1840, the same birthday of his mother's owner's son, James Milton Loring, for whom Turner was named. His father, John Turner, a well-known "horse doctor" in St. Louis, purchased his wife for four hundred dollars and young James for fifty dollars, with the help of a white physician, who spread word that James's mother had an injury that would cause her hand to be amputated.

Turner's education began in clandestine schools in St. Louis in defiance of state law that prohibited the education of African Americans. Turner was later admitted to Oberlin College Preparatory School. He left before graduation to return to St. Louis after his father's death to help support his mother and sister.

During the Civil War, Turner served Union Colonel Madison Miller. Turner was present at many early Civil War skirmishes and battles, including Camp Jackson, Wilson's Creek, and Shiloh. Turner's assistance and loyalty to the well-connected Miller led to many opportunities. Immediately after the war, Miller's brother-in-law Governor Thomas Fletcher appointed Turner assistant

superintendent of schools. Turner was directed to establish freedman schools in Missouri. He was later appointed by the Kansas City School Board to teach in the state's first free school for African Americans. During this same period Turner was involved in raising money for the establishment of the Lincoln Institute (now Lincoln University), the first school to offer higher education to African Americans in Missouri.

In 1871, President Ulysses S. Grant appointed Turner ambassador to Liberia, a position he held until 1878. After returning from Liberia, Turner remained active in politics. In 1879, he aided African Americans migrating from the South that were passing through St. Louis. In 1881, Turner organized the Freedman's Oklahoma Association to assist formerly enslaved African Americans of the Cherokee Tribes who had land and oil claims in the Oklahoma Indian Territory.

On November 1, 1915, Turner's fascinating career came to an end after suffering from blood poisoning due to an injury from a tank car explosion in Ardmore, Oklahoma.

$\mathcal{G}$eorge Washington

1817–1905
FARMER AND BUSINESSMAN

$\mathcal{G}$eorge Washington, the founder of Centerville (now Centralia), Washington, was born on August 15, 1817, in Frederick County, Virginia. When his father, who was enslaved, was sold shortly after he was born, his mother gave him to a white family by the name of Cochran, who raised the boy. When he was still very young, the family moved to Ohio and then to Missouri. As an adult, Washington eventually operated several businesses and a sawmill in St. Joseph, Missouri.

Washington struggled with the mill—as he had with other businesses under the racial restrictions of the state—and decided to head west in search of greater freedom. The Cochrans joined him and in 1850, they all set out as part of a westward-bound wagon train. After spending three years in Oregon City they crossed the Columbia River into what soon became Washington Territory.

In 1852, Washington and his family began a claim where the Skookumchuck River joins the Chehalis River, becoming the fourth settlers in the area. He cleared the land and began farming. Due to Oregon Territory laws barring settlements by African Americans, Washington had the Cochrans file a claim under the Donation Land Claim Act for six hundred acres in the area. When the area came under Washington Territory, which did not bar African Americans from ownership, the Cochrans deeded the property over to Washington.

While in his fifties, Washington met and married Mary Jane Cornie, a widow of African American and Jewish descent. They recognized their land would be in a central point on the railroad between Kalama, on the Columbia River, and Tacoma, on Puget Sound, and decided to start a town. Over supper at the dinner table the couple laid out two thousand lots, setting aside sites for parks and churches. On January 8, 1875, the Washingtons filed papers for their town, which they called Centerville. In 1883, at the suggestion of settlers, the town's name was changed to Centralia, and it was incorporated in 1886.

The town thrived, and by 1889, when Washington became a state, Centralia's population was nearing one thousand. Washington continued to be actively involved in civic and business affairs until his death on August 26, 1905. The mayor of Centralia proclaimed a day of mourning and requested all businesses to be closed during the funeral. A park on Pearl and Harrison streets, in the heart of the town, is named for Washington.

Cathay Williams
(a.k.a., William Cathay)

1842–between 1892 and 1900
FEMALE BUFFALO SOLDIER

athay Williams was the only woman known to serve in the US Army prior to the official induction of women. Born into slavery in Independence, Missouri, in 1842 to a free father and an enslaved mother named Martha, Williams was owned by William Johnson, a wealthy farmer. Williams and her family were taken to Jefferson City when she was very young. Johnson died there around the start of the Civil War.

When the Union soldiers came to Jefferson City, Williams and other African Americans were freed and taken to Little Rock, Arkansas. There, Williams served General Philip Sheridan and his staff as a cook. She was later recruited to Washington to serve as a cook and laundress. While traveling with the troops she witnessed the Shenandoah Valley raids in Virginia. After leaving Virginia, she traveled to Iowa and then to St. Louis.

When the Civil War ended, Williams found herself on her own, eager to become financially independent. On November 15, 1866, she enlisted at Jefferson Barracks in St. Louis as William Cathay, a man, and was assigned to the 38th US Infantry, a designated segregated African American unit. Her enlistment was possible only because a medical examination was not required.

On October 1, 1867, Williams' unit, Company A, arrived at Fort Williams in New Mexico. Her company protected miners and

Photo courtesy of Angela DaSilva

traveling immigrants from Apache attacks. By 1868, Williams had grown tired of military life, so she feigned illness. At Fort Bayard, she was examined by a post surgeon, who discovered Williams was a woman. Williams was discharged on October 14, 1868.

Williams then traveled to Pueblo, Colorado, where she earned a living as a cook and laundress. She married but soon parted from her mate after she had him arrested for stealing her property. She moved on to Las Animus and later to Trinidad, Colorado.

After a long illness, in 1891, Williams applied for a pension based on her military service. The application was denied after an examination by an assigned pension board physician. It is believed she died sometime between 1892 and 1900 in Colorado.

$\mathcal{Y}$ork

1772–Death Unknown

EXPLORER OF THE LOUISIANA TERRITORY
WITH LEWIS AND CLARK

$\mathcal{I}$n the spring of 1804, the United States launched the Lewis and Clark Expedition, its most ambitious exploration. In two years, the party covered more than eight thousand miles, traveling through Missouri, Kansas, Nebraska, Iowa, North and South Dakota, Montana, Idaho, Washington, and Oregon. Members of the expedition were the first non-natives to explore the land acquired by President Thomas Jefferson from Napoleon in the Louisiana Purchase Treaty—and beyond.

Many Americans have heard how the Shoshone woman, Sacajawea, proved invaluable to the expedition. However, little is mentioned of York, Clark's enslaved Black man and one of the expedition's most important members.

York's contributions to the expedition included his remarkable skills in trail blazing, hunting, fishing, and swimming. The ability of both Lewis and Clark to deal fairly with the Indians and to gain their confidence was revealed time and again during the two years of the expedition, but for many of the tribes, York was the main attraction. He often engaged the interest of the Indians as they assembled in council with the expedition leaders. Messages from Indian tribes went from Sacajawea to her husband to York, and then to Lewis and Clark. The Nez Perce and other tribes that

encountered the Black explorer called him "Tse-mook-tse-mook to-to-kean," which means "Black white man."

When the party returned to St. Louis in September 1806, York was admired and appreciated by all, but he didn't receive any rewards. The other explorers received double pay and land for their services. For more than two years, York had faced the perils of the wilderness, saved Clark's life and that of others, nursed Clark's wounds, guided the expedition, and hunted for food. In return, he once again became Clark's enslaved property.

York was born into slavery around 1772 on the Clark family plantation in Caroline County, Virginia, around the same time as William Clark. After the expedition, when York asked for his freedom, his request was denied.

$\mathcal{H}$iram Young

1812–1882
BUSINESS OWNER

$\mathcal{T}$he story of Hiram Young is one of inspiration, a story of how one individual triumphed over adversity and left behind a powerful legacy for future generations. Young was born into slavery around 1812 in Tennessee and came to Missouri with his owner George Young, who settled in Green County.

With his knowledge of carpentry—and his considerable skill at it—by 1847 Young had saved enough money to purchase freedom for himself and his wife. Legend has it that Young purchased his wife's freedom before his own, because he knew their children would be free if their mother was no longer enslaved.

Young then moved to Liberty, Missouri, in Clay County, and later to Independence in Jackson County, the "outfitting center" for the Santa Fe Trail. Young began making yokes and wagons for hauling government freight across the Plains. By 1860, Young's business had become one of the largest in Jackson County. He employed some fifty or sixty workers in his shop on his 460-acre farm, including several enslaved and freed Blacks and Irish immigrants. The shop produced thousands of yokes and more than eight hundred wagons a year. The 1860 Census shows Young owned $36,000 of real property, $20,000 of personal property, and several enslaved Blacks of his own.

The Civil War interrupted Young's business, and in 1861, he and his family were among the many who fled to Fort Leavenworth. Once in Kansas, he continued his business on a much smaller scale until after the war. In the late 1860s, Young and his family returned to Independence only to find their farm and business in ruins.

Young went to work rebuilding the business and also opened a mill. Young then sued the US government for damages to his property as a result of the war. Neither Young nor his wife were alive to see the outcome of the suit. He died in 1882 and his wife died in 1896. In 1907, their lawsuit was denied.

Joseph Penny

Pioneer and Community Founder
Birth and death dates unknown

After the Civil War, during Reconstruction, many African Americans traveled to different parts of the country in search of a better life. One of those individuals was Joseph Penny, who left Kentucky and found his way to Saline County, Missouri. Once in Saline County he worked as a tenant farmer and saved enough money to purchase eight acres of land south of Marshall for $160.00. This was the beginning of a community that became known as Pennytown.

Penny was followed by other African American farmers, many former slaves and their kin, who purchased more land in the Salt Fork Township until they owned nearly one-third of the land. Soon they developed their own township. The residents developed several programs to help themselves, such as the men helping each other during hog-killing time and wood chopping; and the women sharing the rug making, clothes sewing, and baking. A community fund was developed to assist with the cost of the care of the sick. It was reported to be the largest African American community in Central Missouri.

It is believed Pennytown's peak population was near 1,000. Around 1900, there were approximately 40 families living in the community.

After World War II, the community began to lose its population as Blacks began to move to Marshall and other cities and towns for better-paying jobs and an improved standard of living. In 2020, the only remaining building from the former settlement was the Free Will Baptist Church of Pennytown.

$\mathcal{S}$ylvia Stark
Canadian Woman Pioneer
1839–1943

$\mathcal{S}$ylvia Estes Stark was born in Clay County, Missouri, to enslaved parents in 1838. Her brother Jackson, sister Agnes, and mother, Hannah, were owned by a different owner than her father, Howard. Once gold was discovered in California in 1848, her father's owner sent Howard and his sons to explore opportunities to sell cattle. Sylvia's father remained in California mining for gold. He earned enough money to purchase the family's freedom and a 40-acre farm. He then returned back to Missouri to reunite his family. Finding Missouri not accepting of free Blacks, the family headed for California. After six months they settled outside Placerville, a mining town near Sacramento.

In 1855 Sylvia married Louis Stark. The couple prospered. When the state passed restrictive laws aimed at Blacks, the couple moved to British Columbia. The governor of Vancouver Island offered Blacks "all the rights and protections of citizenship." Sylvia and her husband homesteaded on Salt Spring Island, a sparsely populated wilderness. They later moved across the Island to Fruitvale and built a home. After her husband left to go mining, Sylvia singlehandedly managed the homestead, took care of the livestock, milked the cows, and contended with wild animals stealing her livestock. Along with raising a family, she served as community midwife.

Sylvia died at age 105 in 1944. Her 260 acres were divided among relatives. She was recognized in 2013 as a Canadian Woman Pioneer.

"When the history books are written in future generations, the historians will have to pause and say, 'There lived a great people—a Black people— who injected new meaning and dignity into the veins of civilization.'"
—*Dr. Martin Luther King, Jr.*

$\mathcal{L}$eaders

". . . though it is sometimes very difficult to
imagine our nation totally free of racism and
sexism, my intellect, my heart and my experience
tell me it is actually possible. For the day when
neither exist we must all struggle."
—*James Baldwin*

$\mathcal{M}$alik Ahmed
1951–
$\mathcal{D}$eBorah Ahmed
1955–
BETTER FAMILY LIFE, INC.

$\mathcal{B}$etter Family Life, which began as a dream of its founder Malik Ahmed in 1983, is one of the fastest-growing community development organizations in the St. Louis metropolitan area. Today the nonprofit organization serves more than fifty thousand customers annually; collaborates with more than seven hundred employer-partners and one hundred community, faith-based, and education partners; and employs more than two hundred people in nine locations.

As part of its mission, the organization provides a vast array of programs, ranging from career planning and home ownership to cultural and arts activities. Better Family Life also sponsors several annual events: Black Dance–USA (May), Family Week (August), Unity Ball (November), and Kwanzaa Holiday Expo (December). The organization has received numerous awards, locally and nationally.

In 2005, Better Family Life purchased the 60,000-square-foot Ralph Waldo Emerson Elementary School from the St. Louis Board of Education to house its activities. The historic building is on the National Register of Historic Places.

Ahmed was born in Harlem in 1951. He has traveled and lectured throughout the United States and abroad on issues pertinent to the growth and development of families and communities. As a Peace Corps volunteer in the 1970s, he worked for three years as an urban planner in the West African country of Mali. He holds a bachelor's degree in economics from Herbert H. Lehman College and a master's degree in public administration and policy analysis from Southern Illinois University at Edwardsville.

DeBorah Ahmed, Malik's wife and business partner, is senior vice president of cultural programs at the Better Family Life Cultural Center and Museum. She was born in St. Louis in 1955 and has a bachelor's degree in anthropology from Grinnell College and a master's in policy analysis from Southern Illinois University at Edwardsville. The founding artistic director of Rhythms in Anoa Dance Theatre is also a published author, talk-show host, university and college lecturer, dance performer and choreographer, and jewelry designer.

Charles Alfred Anderson

1907–1994
AVIATOR, METEOROLOGIST

Charles Alfred Anderson, America's first African American PhD meteorologist known as the "The Father of Black Aviation," was born August 13, 1910, on a farm in University City, Missouri. Anderson graduated from Sumner High School as valedictorian and continued his education at Lincoln University in Jefferson City, Missouri. He earned a bachelor's degree in science and a master's degree in meteorology from the University of Chicago, and a second master's degree in chemistry from the Polytechnic Institute of Brooklyn, where he was the first African-American student to earn a degree. Anderson then earned a PhD from Massachusetts Institute of Technology (MIT).

Anderson developed a deep interest in airplanes and flight at an early age. When he was thirteen he applied to the Drexel Institute Aviation School but was denied admission because of his race. When he joined the army to become a pilot, he again was rejected because of his race. Anderson was not deterred. At the age of twenty-two, he taught himself to fly in a used plane purchased with his savings and money he borrowed from friends and relatives. In 1929, he was the first African American to receive a pilot's license. He earned his commercial pilot's license in 1932 and an air transport pilot certification in 1933.

Anderson and a friend made the first round-trip transcontinental flight by Black pilots, flying from Atlantic City to Los

Angeles and back, using a road map and without the aid of parachutes, radios, and flight instruments. The two pilots also became the first to use a land plane to fly from Miami to the Bahamas.

In 1940, Anderson was hired at the Tuskegee Institute as chief flight instructor, to train pilots. One year later, First Lady Eleanor Roosevelt took a special interest in the program and asked to fly with Anderson. Their flight helped lead to the eventual creation of the "Tuskegee Experiment" and the Tuskegee Airmen of World War II.

Anderson died on April 13, 1994, at his home after a long fight with cancer.

$\mathcal{J}$et Banks

1924–2003
STATE SENATOR

$\mathcal{J}$. B. "Jet" Banks, a powerful African American politician, served in the Missouri Legislature for three decades. A sharecropper's son, J. Bernard Banks was born in 1924 in Hermondale, a small town in Southeast Missouri's Bootheel, where he attended public schools. After graduation he enrolled at Lincoln University in Jefferson City and graduated with a bachelor's degree in mathematics with a minor in physics. Banks did graduate work in the fields of business and public administration at Saint Louis University and Washington University. In 1989, he was awarded an honorary doctor of law degree from Lincoln University and an honorary doctorate of Humane Letters from Harris-Stowe State University.

Banks was elected to the Missouri House of Representatives in 1968 from the 54th and 80th Districts in St. Louis, and he served four terms. He was elected for his first term in the Missouri Senate in 1976, representing the 5th District of St. Louis. Banks was the first African American lawmaker to be elected assistant majority floor leader by the Democratic Caucuses of both the House and Senate. In 1988, Banks's experience and dedication were recognized by his colleagues when they elected him senate majority leader, making him the first African American elected to one of the four top leadership posts in the Missouri Assembly. In 1990, he was chosen by acclamation by his colleagues for a second term. Following his third term in this position, in 1995, he was

HARRIS-STOWE STATE UNIVERSITY

J. B. "JET" BANKS
MEMORIAL PARK

elected for an unprecedented fourth term as majority leader.

In the 1970s, Banks shepherded legislation that brought Harris-Stowe, a historically Black St. Louis college, into the state's higher education system. Banks was known for using theatrics to make his case. In 1995, he strapped toy six-shooters under his suit coat to mock backers of a measure that would have legalized concealed guns.

Banks's colorful political career came to an end in 1995, due to poor health and several legal issues. He died in 2003 of natural causes. Two parks, one at Harris-Stowe State University and one on the north side of the city across from Vashon High School, have been named to honor Banks.

$\mathcal{F}$reeman R. Bosley Jr.

1954–
MAYOR AND ATTORNEY

$\mathcal{F}$eeman R. Bosley Jr. made history in 1993, when he became the first African American mayor in St. Louis. Before becoming the forty-third mayor of the city, Bosley was the first African American selected to hold the office of St. Louis circuit clerk for the 22nd Judicial Circuit, a position he held for ten years. Bosley also was the first African American chairman of the Democratic Party in St. Louis City.

As mayor, Bosley accomplished a great deal beginning early in his administration, when the Great Flood of 1993 occurred. He also played a major role in the passing of two property tax increases, in helping to organize the $70 million bailout of Trans World Airlines, and in assisting in the Los Angeles Rams football team's move to St. Louis from Anaheim, California. Bosley also was the first St. Louis mayor to speak at the city's annual Gay and Lesbian Pride Celebration, and he reportedly appointed the first openly gay or lesbian person as a city official. In 1997, Bosley lost his bid for a second term when he was defeated by Clarence Harmon.

Bosley was born in St. Louis on July 20, 1954. He attended St. Louis Public Schools and graduated from Central High School. At Saint Louis University, he received a BA degree in political science and urban affairs. He continued his education at Saint Louis University's Law School, where he received his JD degree.

ST. LOUIS CITY HALL, PHOTO BY JOHN A. WRIGHT, JR.

While in law school, Bosley was president of the Black Student Alliance and the Black-American Law Student Association.

Bosley presently heads his own law firm, Bosley and Associates, LLC.

$\mathcal{E}$dward Bouchet

1852–1918

First African American PhD

$\mathcal{E}$dward Bouchet, one of Sumner High School's early and outstanding teachers, was the first African American to earn a PhD from an American university, the first African American to graduate from Yale University, and the first African American to be nominated to Phi Beta Kappa. Bouchet completed his dissertation in Yale's physics PhD program in 1876.

Of four children, Bouchet was the only son, born September 15, 1852 to William and Susan Cooley Bouchet in New Haven, Connecticut. He attended Artisan Street Colored School, one of three schools open to African Americans. This ungraded school had one teacher, who played a crucial role in developing Bouchet's academic abilities and talents. He attended New Haven High School from 1866 to 1868 and then Hopkins Grammar School, a private institute that prepared young men for the classical and scientific departments at Yale College, where he finished first in his class. He entered Yale College in 1870 and graduated in four years, ranking sixth in a class of 124.

After graduation Bouchet was unable to find a teaching position. In 1876, he moved to Philadelphia, where he taught physics and chemistry at the Institute for Colored Youth (later renamed Cheyney University) for twenty-six years. When the institute moved in the direction of industrial education during

SUMNER HIGH SCHOOL, PHOTO
COURTESY OF THE WESTERN
HISTORICAL MANUSCRIPT COLLECTION,
UNIVERSITY OF MISSOURI–ST. LOUIS

the height of the W.E.B. DuBois–Booker T. Washington debate over the need for collegiate vs. industrial education for African Americans, Bouchet resigned from the school.

In 1902, Bouchet moved to St. Louis to teach math and physics at Sumner High School. He then spent seven months as the business manager for the Provident Hospital, followed by a stint as a US Customs postal inspector at the Louisiana Purchase Exposition in St. Louis. After leaving St. Louis, Bouchet held teaching and administrative positions in Ohio and Virginia until he was forced to retire because of arteriosclerosis. He returned to New Haven, where he died in his boyhood home in 1918 at the age of sixty-six. Bouchet had no wife or children.

Nathaniel Bruce

1868–1942

EDUCATOR AND FOUNDER OF BARTLETT AGRICULTURAL AND INDUSTRIAL SCHOOL

In 1907, Nathaniel C. Bruce, the son of formerly enslaved parents, established the Bartlett Agricultural and Industrial School, later known as Dalton Vocational School near Dalton in Chariton County, Missouri. Bruce, a former student of Booker T. Washington at Tuskegee Institute in Alabama, believed in Washington's approach to educating African Americans through vocational and agricultural training in order to become financially independent. He often called his school "the Tuskegee of the Mid-West."

Bruce was born in 1868 on a farm near Danville, Virginia, and attended the Halifax County Public Schools. He left home when he was fourteen to attend the Shaw Normal and Industrial High School in Raleigh, North Carolina. After gradation, he furthered his education at Shaw University, where he received his bachelor's degree. He continued his education at several other Eastern institutions along with Tuskegee Institute.

Bruce began his career in St. Joseph, Missouri, where he worked as principal of an African American high school. In 1907, he made a decision to establish the Bartlett Agricultural and Industrial School. The school opened in a rented log barn located in the Missouri River bottom. The land flooded in 1908 and 1909, destroying all the crops. The school was moved to a higher location and further developed with the assistance of white benefactors. In 1913 the efforts of Bruce and his staff began

to pay off. In 1914, the school won the annual Missouri Ruralist contest for the most corn per acre, despite a statewide drought, and won again the following year along with finishing second nationally in corn production at the Panama-Pacific International Exposition in San Francisco. By 1920 over five hundred students had been enrolled at the school since its beginning, with more than two hundred graduating.

In 1924 Bruce left the school to become state inspector of Negro Schools. The school continued to grow and was taken over by the state and placed under the control of the University of Missouri until 1929, when control was transferred to Lincoln University. The school closed after the 1954 *Brown v. Board of Education* case, in which the US Supreme Court ruled segregated education unconstitutional. By 1956, students from Chariton and surrounding counties were attending schools in their home districts.

$\mathcal{J}$ames Buford

1944–2019

URBAN LEAGUE PRESIDENT AND CEO AND CIVIL RIGHTS
ADVOCATE

$\mathcal{J}$ames H. Buford—past president and CEO of the St. Louis Metropolitan Urban League, founder of the St. Louis Black Leadership Roundtable, and 2013 St. Louis Citizen of the Year—guided the Urban League for nearly three decades. Under Buford's leadership, the St. Louis Urban League grew to become the fourth largest League in the country with an annual budget that grew from $2.4 million to over $21.6 million, a staff of 84 to 190, and from four locations to 10 with 30 different programs serving over 70,000 individuals. The St. Louis Metropolitan Urban League also became the first League in the country to gain a five-star rating and one of two Leagues in the country with service sites in two states, Missouri and Illinois.

Buford, while at the head of the Urban League, was one of the area's most visible and vocal African American leaders. He oversaw services from job training to home weatherization, early childhood education to emergency food donations, and violence prevention programs to housing counseling. As an advocate for social and economic parity and spokesperson on behalf of Urban League constituents, he sat on more than twenty boards and commissions. In carrying out his duties he marched and went to jail for social justice on behalf of the less fortunate. Due to his sincere and principled efforts he has received numerous awards and gained the respect of community, state, and national leaders. He has been recognized with appointments from Presidents

Ronald Reagan and George H. W. Bush, Missouri Governor Matt Blunt, and St. Louis Mayor Francis Slay.

Born in 1944 in St. Louis to James Buford and Myrtle Margaret Brown Buford, he attended Visitation and St. Marks elementary schools. After graduation, he attended St. Louis Preparatory Seminary and later transferred and graduated from St. Catherine of Laboure High School. Buford went on to receive a bachelor's degree in human service administration from Elizabeth College, Elizabethtown, Pennsylvania. He holds honorary doctorates of humane letters from Harris-Stowe State University, Webster University, Eden Theological Seminary, University of Missouri–St. Louis, and Fontbonne University.

Buford retired in 2013, after twenty-eight years of a stellar career at the Urban League. Prior to joining the League he was state director of jobs for Missouri graduates. He and his wife, Susan, lived in the city of St. Louis. They have two sons, James Jr. and Jason.

George Washington Carver

1861–1943

SCIENTIST AND EDUCATOR

While the average person viewed peanuts simply as a food, George Washington Carver saw their potential. Over time, he developed 325 different products from the peanut, including face powder, ink, butter, coffee, vinegar, soap, and wood stains. He also created 118 different products from the sweet potato.

Carver was born enslaved in 1861 on Moses Carver's plantation in Diamond Grove, Missouri. His father died in an accident before he was born, and as an infant, Carver and his mother were kidnapped by a Confederate slave raider. The raiders returned the boy in exchange for a horse, and he was raised by Moses Carver and his wife. Because he was a sickly child, Carver was unable to do heavy work and instead spent much of his time wandering in the nearby woods, collecting flowers and plants.

At age ten, Carver went to school in Neosho, Missouri, where he lived with a Black family. He put himself through grammar school and high school in Minneapolis, Kansas, and later through one year at Simpson College in Iowa, where he was the first African American to attend the school. With the help of his art teacher, Carver was accepted at Iowa Agricultural College in 1891. Due to his outstanding work, he was requested to remain at the college as an assistant instructor after graduation.

In 1896, Booker T. Washington invited Carver to head the agricultural department at Tuskegee Normal and Industrial

Institute in Alabama. There, he developed a system of crop rotation. He first planted peanuts, which replenished nitrogen in the soil, followed by cotton the next year, to keep the soil rich and improve the harvest. The system was so successful that peanuts soon flooded the market, prompting Carver to discover many uses for the legumes. His methods also led to greater diversification, enabling him to develop many uses for the sweet potato.

Because of Carver's success he received numerous employment offers and honors. He was awarded honorary doctorates from Selma University and the University of Rochester. He received an appointment to the Royal Society of Arts in London, and the National Association for the Advancement of Colored People (NAACP) gave Carver the prestigious Spingarn Medal. In 1947, a postage stamp was issued with Carver's image, and his profile appeared on the fifty-cent piece in 1951.

Through it all, Carver remained at Tuskegee, wishing only to improve the lives of African American farmers through his research.

$\mathcal{W}$illiam Lacy Clay Sr.

1931–

MISSOURI'S FIRST AFRICAN AMERICAN US REPRESENTATIVE,
AUTHOR, HISTORIAN, CIVIL RIGHTS ACTIVIST

$\mathcal{W}$illiam Lacy Clay Sr., the first African American elected to the US House of Representatives from Missouri, was born in St. Louis in 1931, to Irving and Luella (Hyatt) Clay. Clay recounts that his first political epiphany occurred in 1949, after he was arrested and pushed by police to confess to a crime for which he had no connection.

Thanks to an aunt who worked for one of the police commissioners, he was released after she telephoned her employer. Clay later recalled that it was at that point he knew that survival and political influence were inseparable in American society.

Clay was an outstanding student, and at the age of thirteen he began working as a janitor in a clothing store, where he later became a tailor. After high school Clay entered Saint Louis University, where he earned bachelor's degrees in history and political science in 1953. Following graduation, he was drafted and served in the army from 1953 to 1955. While in the service, he responded to racial discrimination by leading a boycott of the barbershop on base, to protest its policy of serving African Americans only one day a week.

Later, Clay returned to St. Louis and briefly worked as a real estate broker. In 1959, he won his first elective office—that of St. Louis alderman—a position he held until 1964. As an elected official, he continued to push for civil rights and participated in a

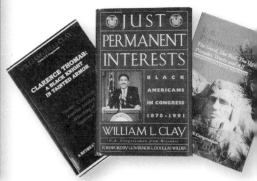

WILLIAM L. CLAY SR.'S BOOKS, PHOTO COURTESY OF JOHN A. WRIGHT JR.

series of protests. In 1963, he served 112 days in jail for participating in a demonstration against the hiring practices of Jefferson Bank in St. Louis. Between 1961 and 1964, Clay also served as a business representative for the city employees' union, and in 1966–67, he was the education coordinator for a local steamfitters' union.

In 1968, Clay won the Democratic Primary nomination for Missouri's First Congressional District and he won the seat in the general election. He went on to serve for sixteen terms before retiring in 2001. While in Congress, Clay was one of the founding members of the Congressional Black Caucus. He also helped author the Tax Reform Act of 1986 and sponsored legislation for the protection of labor unions' negotiation rights with employers, as well as mandatory notification of plant closings, and parental and medical leave.

For his stellar career Clay has been honored in his district with numerous awards, which include his name on the downtown diamond walk of fame, a post office, street, Early Childhood Development and Parenting Education Center at Harris-Stowe State University, and the Center for Nanoscience at University of Missouri–St. Louis.

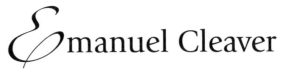

$\mathcal{E}$manuel Cleaver

1944–

POLITICIAN, MINISTER, CLERGYMAN, AND PASTOR

$\mathcal{E}$manuel Cleaver—US Representative for Missouri's 5th Congressional District, former mayor of Kansas City, and a Methodist minister—moved to Kansas City, Missouri, in the 1960s, where he founded a branch of the Southern Christian Leadership Conference. Once there, Cleaver became deeply involved in the community. He enrolled in the St. Paul School of Theology, where he received his master of divinity degree.

In 1972, Cleaver became pastor of St. James United Methodist Church. The church presently has the largest African American congregation of any United Methodist Church in the state. Because of his success as a congregation developer and church builder, Cleaver now assists Missouri Bishop Robert Schnase to build congregations, especially in African American communities.

In 1991, after serving twelve years on the city council, Cleaver was elected as Kansas City's first African American mayor. During his eight-year tenure as mayor, Cleaver had many successes. He brought a number of major corporations to the city, oversaw the building of the South Midtown Roadway and the reconstruction and beautification of Brush Creek, assisted with the 18th and Vine Redevelopment, helped get the new American Royal Stadium built, and helped establish a Family Division of the Municipal Court.

As a member of the Democratic Party, Cleaver was elected US Representative for Missouri's 5th Congressional District,

US STATES HOUSE OF REPRESENTATIVES,
PHOTO COURTESY OF THE UNITED STATES GOVERNMENT

PHOTO COURTESY OF EMANUEL
CLEAVER

which included virtually all of Kansas City south of the Missouri River and most of the city's suburbs in Jackson County. Cleaver is credited with introduction of the ambitious Green Impact Zone project. Aimed at the urban core, this project received $125 million in American Recovery and Reinvestment funds to make a high-crime area the "greenest" piece of urban geography in the world. The project includes home weatherization, rehabbing bridges, jobs for Green Zone residents, and many community improvement projects. In 2010, Cleaver was unanimously elected the 20th chairman of the Congressional Black Caucus of the 112th Congress.

Cleaver was born in Waxahachie, Texas, on October 26, 1944, the son of Marie McKnight and Lucky G. Cleaver. He grew up in Wichita Falls, Texas. Cleaver is the recipient of five honorary doctoral degrees and he holds a bachelor's degree from Prairie View A&M University.

ois D. Conley

1947–

*S*tarting with a dream and an idea to create a museum that would help develop a community of lifelong learners who explore, experience, and embrace Missouri's rich and enduring African American heritage, Lois D. Conley opened the Black World History Wax Museum in 1997. It was the second of its kind in the country. In 2008, the name was changed to the Griot Museum of Black History, which Conley felt better expressed the museum's mission.

The Griot uses life-size wax figures along with other art, artifacts, and memorabilia to interpret the stories of African Americans with a regional connection to St. Louis who also have contributed to the country's development. Visitors may learn about Josephine Baker, Miles Davis, Percy Green, Dred and Harriet Scott, and many others. Traveling exhibits often find a home at the Griot as well. The museum also engages in a variety of educational outreach programs, which include special education projects, lectures, and cultural events.

Conley is a native of St. Louis and a graduate of Vashon High School. After high school she earned a bachelor's degree in communications and a master's degree in education from Saint Louis University. She also holds a graduate certificate in museum studies from the University of Missouri–St. Louis.

Conley has dedicated many years to researching African American history and has consulted with a variety of organizations—including the National Parks Service and the Royal Tropical Museum in Amsterdam—on the study and exhibition of the Underground Railroad and slavery. Due to her work, Conley has been honored by numerous organizations. She has lectured throughout the region and has before conducted numerous tours of historic African American sites in St. Louis.

Cropperville

1939
SHARECROPPERS' PROTEST SETTLERS

One of the most significant, yet neglected, events in American labor history is the sharecroppers' labor protest held in 1939 in Southeast Missouri. On a cold January morning, more than one thousand sharecroppers, all evicted from their homes, camped out along two state highways with their meager belongings. They wanted the government and their fellow citizens to know how one group of Americans lived. The sharecroppers were protesting a new farm policy—the Agricultural Adjustment Act, part of President Franklin Roosevelt's New Deal Administration. A loophole allowed plantation owners to keep government money they owed the sharecroppers if they let them go and hired new ones to take their place.

Reverend Owen H. Whitfield, an African American minister, organized the protest. Whitfield was a sharecropper and also vice president of the Southern Tenant Farmers Union, whose mission was to work for better conditions for farm workers. He convinced the sharecroppers that the demonstration would draw attention to their plight. Although they were in the frigid cold along the highway, the protesters were refused assistance from the Red Cross, which considered the situation a "manmade disaster." However, day after day the protesters remained along the highway, some with only iron cook stoves for warmth.

Soon they began to draw national attention. Reporters and photographers from national newspapers began to flock to

the area, much to the embarrassment of the state and national governments. Lorenzo Greene, a Lincoln University professor, visited the site and came away horrified. He described the situation to his students, who canceled their spring prom and donated money to help the sharecroppers.

An activist by the name of Fannie Cook organized a citizens' committee to donate money to the sharecroppers. With money from Cook's committee and the students, Whitfield and the sharecroppers bought ninety-three acres near Poplar Bluff, Missouri. Several hundred sharecroppers, both Black and white, moved to the site, which became known as "Cropperville."

The sharecroppers tilled the land, built homes, opened a church and school, and planted a community garden. The federal government got involved and created the Delmo Homes communities, ten villages in the Bootheel for sharecroppers. However, after ten years the community had all but disappeared after many individuals moved on to find better jobs or fight in World War II.

$\mathcal{J}$ulia Davis

1891–1993

EDUCATOR, HISTORIAN, AND PHILANTHROPIST

$\mathcal{I}$n 1974, the St. Louis Public Library broke with tradition by dedicating a library branch in honor of a living person—Julia Davis, a lifelong educator, historian, and philanthropist. Davis was a native of St. Louis and a graduate of Dumas Elementary School, Sumner High, and Normal School. She received her bachelor's degree from Stowe Teachers College in 1937, a master's degree from the University of Iowa in 1942, and an honorary doctorate from the University of Missouri–St. Louis in 1981.

In 1910, Davis began her fifty-one-year teaching career with the St. Louis Public Schools as an apprentice teacher at the Dessalines School. In 1961, she retired from Simmons Elementary School, after teaching there thirty-five years. Throughout her years as a teacher, she was an avid supporter of integrated and inclusive history.

Davis was a tireless community worker and volunteer, an active participant in professional organizations, a recognized researcher in Black history, a Sunday school teacher and church historian, the creator of Negro History Exhibits at the St. Louis Public Library, and a writer of educational and religious plays and pageants.

On the day of her retirement, Davis contributed twenty-five hundred dollars for the establishment of the Julia Davis Fund at the St. Louis Public Library to purchase books and materials

pertaining to African American contributions and achievements.

After her retirement, Davis wrote historical material on the twenty schools named for African Americans in St. Louis. She compiled a calendar of Negro Achievement, finding an event for every day of the year. This project was an outgrowth of a program she wrote for radio station KATZ, titled "Tidbits for Children," which involved short descriptions about local African Americans and their contributions. Davis also served as a researcher for *Heritage of St. Louis*, a textbook used in classrooms in the St. Louis Public School System.

Davis once stated: "Education is the strongest weapon we have for dispelling prejudices and untruths."

$\mathcal{H}$erman Dreer

1889–1981
EDUCATOR, MINISTER, AND HISTORIAN

$\mathcal{A}$n outstanding educator, minister, writer, and historian, Herman Dreer was the grandson of slaves. He was born in 1888 in Washington, D.C., where he attended elementary and high school. After graduation, he enrolled in Bowdoin College in Brunswick, Maine, where he graduated magna cum laude and Phi Beta Kappa in 1910.

Dreer taught at Virginia Theological Seminary in Lynchburg, Virginia, and while there he earned master's degrees in Latin and theology. Throughout his career, Dreer continued studying. In 1942, he received a master's degree in sociology from the University of Chicago, and in 1955, at age sixty-seven, he earned a PhD in sociology. His dissertation—"Negro Leadership in St. Louis: A Study in Race Relations"—provides valuable insight into the city's African American community during the period of the study.

Dreer moved to St. Louis in 1914 to teach at Sumner High School. During his time there, he taught English, history, sociology, chemistry, Greek, and Latin. One of Dreer's major ambitions was to increase the availability of higher education in the African American community, something he knew about firsthand. His postgraduate sociology degrees were from the University of Chicago because he was denied admission to Saint Louis University and Washington University due to his race. In 1935, he reopened Douglass University, which originally was established in 1926 by B. F. Bowles. Dreer supported the

Douglass University

Offers
STANDARD COURSES
In Liberal Arts, Religion, Business Administration and Law
Leading to the Degrees, A.B., B.Th., and LL.B.

EXCELLENT FACULTY

FINE STUDENT FACILITIES
Study in Saint Louis, the City of Opportunity.
For Further Information Write Freeman L. Martin, Pres.
ENROLL NOW FOR

Summer & Fall Courses

Responsible Homes Near the University Under the
Supervision of the University for Out-of-Town Students.

Copyright, 1937
By DOUGLASS UNIVERSITY PRESS
St. Louis, Mo.

establishment of Stowe Teachers College in 1940 and he worked for the integration of Washington University in 1948.

Dreer promoted and stressed the study of African American history. He was a life member of the Association for the Study of Negro Life and History. He wrote a weekly column on Black history for the *St. Louis Argus* newspaper, and in 1950 he edited *American Literature by Negro Authors*. He also researched and helped to finance the *Shelley v. Kraemer* civil rights case in 1948, in which the US Supreme Court considered race-restrictive covenants in housing. Dreer served as chair of the citizens committee. While teaching, Dreer wrote and edited extensively, publishing articles in a wide variety of professional journals and magazines and editing a number of publications as well, most notably the *St. Louis Tribune*, a weekly newspaper. He also wrote the history of the Omega Psi Phi Fraternity, multiple plays, and two novels. His second novel, *The Tie That Binds*, published in 1958, describes an ambitious, idealistic young man who attempts to improve social and racial conditions in St. Louis.

Dreer retired from Harris Teachers College at the age of seventy but continued to teach at other universities in Kansas and Illinois and work in the community. He died in 1981, at the age of ninety-three.

$\int$ister Mary Antona Ebo

1924–2017

Nun, Hospital Administrator, and Civil Rights Pioneer

$\int$n 1965, when Sister Mary Antona Ebo heard the news of a brutal attack by state troopers and police on peaceful voting rights demonstrators attempting to cross Selma's Edmund Pettus Bridge, she felt the need to become involved. The nun received permission from her order to journey to Selma, where along with five nuns and several clergymen, she protested the attack and joined Dr. Martin Luther King Jr. in his second attempt to cross the bridge.

As the only African American nun among the marchers, Sister Ebo soon found herself at the front of the march. Her participation drew national attention and made her one of the icons of the civil rights movement.

Sister Ebo's life was that of a pioneer and fighter. She was born Elizabeth Louise in Bloomington, Illinois, on April 24, 1924, to Daniel and Louise Teale Ebo. Her mother died when Sister Ebo was just four years old, and shortly afterwards her father lost his job and the family home. The family's three children were placed in the McLean County Home for Colored Children, in Bloomington, where Sister Ebo was baptized a Catholic. She attended Holy Trinity High School there and was the school's first African American graduate.

Ebo prayed for a vocation and applied for admission to the local Catholic school of nursing in Bloomington. Her application was rejected because of her race. She then applied to and was

SISTER MARY ANTONA EBO AT CAMPUS MINISTRY OF XAVIER UNIVERSITY IN LOUISIANA, PHOTO COURTESY OF JOHN A. WRIGHT, JR.

accepted at the St. Mary's Infirmary School of Nursing in St. Louis, as part of the United States Cadet Nurse Corps. In 1946, Sister Ebo became one of the first three African American women to join the Sisters of Mary (now known as the Franciscan Sisters of Mary). In 1967, she was selected director of St. Clare's Catholic Hospital in Baraboo, Wisconsin, the first African American woman executive director of a hospital in the United States. She also served as executive director of the Wisconsin Conference of Catholic Hospitals.

Until her death in 2017, Sister Ebo served as a spokesperson for civil rights causes; to many she was known as the "Face of Civil Rights." For her work she received numerous honors and awards, which include the 2012 Lifetime Achiever in Health Care from the *St. Louis American* Foundation; honorary doctorates from Aquinas Institute of Theology, Loyola University–Chicago, College of New Rochelle in New York, Saint Louis University, and the University of Missouri–St. Louis; and the Harriet Tubman Award from the National Black Sisters Conference, which she helped found and later served as president.

Walter Farmer

1867–1944

ATTORNEY

On June 14, 1889, at Washington University's commencement program, the loudest applause of the day came when the student graduating cum laude was asked to stand. That student was Walter Moran Farmer, the first African American to graduate from the university. The lone Black candidate for a degree in law (LLB) was described as "neither nervous or self-conscious." After five years of study, Farmer was graduating with the second-highest honors in his class.

Farmer was born in Brunswick, Missouri, in Charlton County, on January 16, 1867, just two years after emancipation in Missouri. His family was assisted in his raising by a white family whom they had served during the Civil War. There was a boy in the white family that was around the same age as Farmer, and he and Farmer became best friends. The boy went to high school, and Farmer went to Lincoln Institute in Jefferson City, where he graduated in 1884.

When Farmer returned to Brunswick, he was prepared to seek employment as a teacher. His white friend was ready to enter the University of Missouri, which Farmer had no chance of entering. Because of their friendship, his friend began soliciting funds in town to send Farmer off to a college where his color would not handicap him. The money was raised and Farmer came to St. Louis, where he entered Washington University.

At that time the university was a developing institution, founded by liberal and anti-slavery backers a few years prior to

WASHINGTON UNIVERSITY, PHOTO
BY JOHN A. WRIGHT, SR.

the Civil War. After graduating, Farmer practiced law in St. Louis. He rose quickly in his profession and received an appointment as special commissioner to try certain state cases in the circuit court.

Farmer was recognized as a civic leader. He helped organize the national day of "humiliation, fasting, and prayer" in 1892 that was developed to educate whites about the realities of Black life in the hope of making things better for Blacks. On that day, fifteen hundred Blacks solemnly gathered in St. Louis for what they called a "lamentation day." Farmer also was a founding member of the Anniversary Club, one of the oldest, if not *the* oldest, African American male social clubs in Missouri. He also was an active member of Central Baptist Church.

In 1905, the year after the World's Fair in St. Louis, Farmer moved to Chicago, where he practiced law until a year before his death in 1944.

$\mathcal{F}$rankie Freeman

1916–2018
ATTORNEY

$\mathcal{F}$rankie Muse Freeman, the first woman appointed to the United States Commission on Civil Rights (1964 to 1979) was born to William and Maude Beatrice Smith Muse, in Danville, Virginia, in 1916. She attended Westmoreland School and at age sixteen enrolled in Hampton Institute. In 1944, Frankie was admitted to Howard University Law School and received her law degree three years later, placing second in her class.

After graduation Freeman applied to several firms. Receiving no reply, she decided to establish her own private practice. She began with pro bono, divorce, and criminal cases. After two years, Freeman began working in civil rights as legal counsel to the National Association for the Advancement of Colored People (NAACP) legal team that filed a suit in 1949 against the St. Louis Board of Education. Two students at a segregated high school in St. Louis sought access to an aero-mechanics course only offered at the white high school. The court ruled that the school board had to allow the students admission or provide such a course at their school.

Rather than allow the students to enroll in the white high school, the board closed the program down. This court ruling led Freeman to be the lead attorney in the landmark case *Davis et. al. v. The St. Louis Housing Authority*, where she was successful in getting a ruling against discrimination in public housing.

Freeman's drive for equality brought her to the attention of

President Lyndon B. Johnson, who nominated her to the US Civil Rights Commission, which investigated voter discrimination and made recommendations on federal policies, including some written as part of the Voter Rights Act of 1965. Upon her Senate confirmation, Freeman became the first woman named to the commission, on which she remained for sixteen years.

Freeman returned to St. Louis, where she continued to practice law. In 1999, long after she had reached retirement age, Freeman was appointed to co-chair an advisory committee to oversee the settlement agreement in the landmark St. Louis school desegregation case.

In 2003, Freeman published her memoir, *A Song of Faith and Hope*. She was past national president of Delta Sigma Theta Sorority.

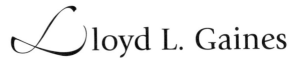

Lloyd L. Gaines

1911–1939
STUDENT

Lloyd Gaines was responsible for bringing about the first in a series of court decisions that culminated in the abandonment of the 1896 "separate but equal" doctrine of *Plessy v. Ferguson.* Gaines filed his suit, *Gaines v. Canada*, after he was denied admission to the University of Missouri Law School because he was an African American. Gaines refused the school's offer to pay his tuition to attend another school in a neighboring state, one that had no racial restrictions.

Instead, Gaines approached the National Association for the Advancement of Colored People (NAACP), which assembled a legal team to assist him. His case was rejected by the Boone County Circuit Court and, on appeal, by the Missouri Supreme Court. But on December 12, 1938, in a landmark decision, the United States Supreme Court ruled 7-2 that the University of Missouri School of Law, then a segregated institution, would have to admit Gaines unless the state could offer him equivalent training elsewhere.

Gaines had publicly announced his intention of entering the University of Missouri the following September. During the 1939 session, however, the Missouri Legislature passed a bill providing $275,000 to establish a law school as part of Lincoln University in Jefferson City. Administrators there found available space in the Poro College building in St. Louis, and the new law school opened with thirty students.

Gaines was not among them. In March 1939, Gaines traveled to Chicago. He left the fraternity house where he was staying to buy some stamps, and he disappeared. Gaines was never seen or heard from again.

Gaines was born in 1911 in Water Valley, Mississippi. He moved with his family to St. Louis when he was fourteen years old. He graduated first in his class from Vashon High School. After attending Stowe Teachers College, Gaines entered Lincoln University in Jefferson City on a $250 scholarship. He made up the difference between the scholarship and tuition by selling magazines on the street. He completed his bachelor's degree with honors and applied for admission to the University of Missouri's Law School.

In 2006, Gaines was granted an honorary posthumous law degree from the University of Missouri, and in 2007, sixty-eight years after his death, the Federal Bureau of Investigation (FBI) agreed to look into the case.

$\mathcal{O}$llie Gates

1932–
BUSINESSMAN

$\mathcal{O}$ne of the names synonymous with Kansas City is Gates and Son's Bar-B-Q. The firm began in 1946, when George W. Gates decided to open a family-owned restaurant, "Gates Ol' Kentucky," at Nineteenth and Vine streets. Gates pooled his resources and created what is now a thriving business. From the early days, the business offered customers a variety of tantalizing barbequed foods and an especially flavorful sauce.

Though he faced a number of setbacks, Gates continued to grow the business until he passed away in 1960. Ollie, the youngest of three children, then took over. Ollie Gates was born in Kansas City in 1932. He graduated from Lincoln High School. Following two years of academic work at Maryland State College, he moved back to the Midwest to attend Lincoln University in Jefferson City, Missouri, so he could work in the family business on weekends. After graduation Gates enlisted in the army as a second lieutenant. He completed the Army School of Engineering and was discharged from active duty as a first lieutenant after serving two years in the US Corps of Engineers.

Gates then returned home to begin building the family business. With a college degree in building construction and invaluable training from the army, young Gates was ready to turn a new page in the history of the business. He designed the layout and features for construction of the company's first ground-up

restaurant in 1956. This heralded the beginning of the Gates Bar-B-Q business model that exists today. There now are six branches of the restaurant.

To ensure success, Gates required all new employees and anyone receiving a promotion to be trained at his Rib Tech, which employed classroom learning techniques. Two themes from the training remain in place today: Service shall be "Fast, Efficient, Courteous, and Correct" (FECC), and "Clean as you go!"

One major reason for the success of Gates and Son's Bar-B-Q has been the sauce, which is manufactured by the restaurant. To meet the growing demand, Gates now plans to sell the sauce at retail grocery stores throughout the nation.

$\mathscr{H}$enry Givens Jr.

1932–
UNIVERSITY PRESIDENT

$\mathscr{H}$enry Givens, a world-class educator, has helped thousands of students achieve their dreams. To accomplish this, he has worn many hats: teacher, principal, state assistant commissioner of urban education, and university president.

Givens also has served as a consultant for the US State Department's American School in Lima, Peru, and has been recognized by more than one hundred national, state, and local organizations. He also has received two honorary doctorates of humane letters.

A native of St. Louis, Givens is a product of the St. Louis Public Schools. After graduating from Sumner High School, he earned a bachelor's degree from Lincoln University, a master's degree from the University of Illinois, and a PhD from Saint Louis University. He pursued postdoctoral administration credentials at Harvard University.

Givens began his career as a teacher in the Webster Groves School District (a suburb of St. Louis) and was named principal of the nation's first prototype magnet school. He later was named assistant to the superintendent of schools. He was the first African American to serve as assistant commissioner of urban education in Missouri, holding the position for five years.

In 1979, Givens was selected as the first president of Harris

PHOTOS COURTESY OF DR. HENRY GIVENS JR.

Teachers College (now Harris-Stowe State University) when it became a part of Missouri's higher educational system. He served the university until he retired in 2011. During his tenure as president, he took the university from a one-building campus with a one-degree program to a seven-building campus offering fourteen degrees. An off-site satellite campus business school also opened, and student enrollment tripled.

During the mid-1980s, Missouri Governor John Ashcroft called on Givens to lead an effort to pull Jefferson City's Lincoln University out of a $3 million deficit. He agreed to work to save his alma mater from financial ruin. During this period, he spent three days a week at Lincoln and three days at Harris-Stowe.

Since 1986, Givens has served as chairman of the Dr. Martin Luther King Jr. State Celebration for Missouri, making it the second-largest celebration in the nation paying tribute to Dr. King.

$\mathcal{L}$orenzo Greene

1899–1988

PROFESSOR, HISTORIAN, AND CIVIL RIGHTS ACTIVIST

$\mathcal{L}$orenzo Johnson Greene—Lincoln University professor, pioneer in African American studies, and civil rights activist—was born on November 16, 1899, in Ansonia, Connecticut. In 1917, he became the first African American to graduate from Ansonia High School. After graduation he went on to receive his bachelor's degree in 1924 from Howard University in Washington, D.C., and his master's degree in history in 1926 from Columbia University in New York.

Two years later, Greene began a long association with Carter G. Woodson, the director of the Association for the Study of Negro Life and History. From 1928 to 1933, Greene served as Woodson's field representative and research assistant. In 1930, the two traveled through Houston and other Southern cities, selling books from Woodson's Associated Publishers that promoted African American history.

In the fall of 1933, Greene joined the faculty of Lincoln University in Jefferson City, Missouri, where he served as instructor and professor of history and where he promoted African American studies until his retirement in 1972. During this time, he continued his own graduate studies and received his doctorate in history from Columbia University in 1942. His dissertation, "The Negro in Colonial New England, 1620-1776," became part of Columbia University's *Studies in History, Economics and Public Law.*

REVISED EDITION

Missouri's
Black Heritage

Lorenzo J. Greene, Gary R. Kremer, Antonio F. Holland

Revised and updated by
Gary R. Kremer and Antonio F. Holland

In 1939, Greene helped bring aid to sharecroppers camped along the highways in Southeast Missouri to protest working conditions in the area. Greene visited the site and then described the horrible situation to his class at Lincoln University. The students canceled their spring prom and donated money to help the sharecroppers. Later, the students sent more money for the sharecroppers to purchase land near Poplar Bluff, Missouri.

Through his membership with the Missouri Association for Social Welfare, Greene worked to end segregation in public accommodations in Jefferson City and St. Louis. In the 1950s, Greene helped to establish the Missouri Human Rights Commission. He also worked on national committees under Presidents Hoover, Eisenhower, and Johnson.

Greene co-authored nine books and wrote many scholarly articles on a variety of topics. His most significant academic work was *Missouri's Black Heritage*, published in 1980 as a collaborative effort with Antonio F. Holland and Gary Kremer. Greene died in Jefferson City on January 24, 1988, leaving as a lasting legacy his works regarding African American history and research.

$\mathcal{P}$ercy Green

1935–
CIVIL RIGHTS ACTIVIST

$\mathcal{W}$hen the final chapter is written on the civil rights movement in St. Louis, the name of Percy Green II will stand out among those working for justice. When Green looked around at the problems in the African American community, he believed that many could be resolved through employment—and he took on the challenge.

On July 14, 1964, Green, along with Richard Daly, members of ACTION, the more progressive members of the Congress of Racial Equality (CORE), climbed the work ladder on the outside of the unfinished Gateway Arch. They then chained themselves to the structure to draw attention to the lack of African American workers employed in the monument's construction. Their protest brought about the federal government's earliest legal tests in America regarding equal employment opportunities for African Americans.

A month after the incident at the Arch, Green and a number of other McDonnell-Douglas Corporation employees were laid off. During the months that followed, the company placed ads in the newspapers looking for workers with the same skills of those who had been laid off. When Green applied for his former job, he was turned down. He filed suit. The landmark outcome of *Percy Green v. McDonnell-Douglas* made it the responsibility of employers to prove their practices were not discriminatory.

Some of the other activities of ACTION, an interracial human-rights protest organization, included deliberately tying up traffic on

the St. Louis highways and passing out leaflets telling drivers that as long as they were stopped, they might think about "how St. Louis is the most racist city in the Union"; demonstrating in churches to point out the responsibility churches had to eradicate racism in employment; picketing in front of business establishments for fair employment; and the unmasking of the Veiled Prophet at the Veiled Prophet Ball, a white society event. Later, the group sponsored a Black Veiled Prophet Afro Festival "in de park" at which a Queen of Human Justice was crowned to mock the Veiled Prophet, "the St. Louis symbol of white racism and oppression," as one flier stated.

Green, a native of the St. Louis Compton Hill area and graduate of Vashon High School, has before paid a high price for protesting discrimination in employment. Reportedly, he was targeted by a government counter-intelligence program that sent poison pen letters and made harassing phone calls to his home.

Dick Gregory

1932–2017

Comedian, Human Rights Activist, and Author

For over five decades, Dick Gregory has used humor drawn from the Black experience in America as a weapon in the struggle of African Americans against racism and discrimination.

Born into poverty in St. Louis in 1932, Richard Clayton Gregory was the second of six children of Presley and Lucille Gregory. As a youngster, he worked to help support the family by delivering packages and groceries and shining shoes in a pool hall. At Sumner High School, he distinguished himself as a track star, winning the Missouri State Mile Championship in 1951. In his senior year, Gregory was elected class president. While a student, he led a protest at the Board of Education regarding overcrowded conditions at the school.

After graduating from Sumner High School, Gregory won an athletic scholarship to Southern Illinois University at Carbondale, where he ran track. He left after two years and entered the army, where he soon found work as a comedian in Special Services shows. Following his stint in the army, Gregory moved to Chicago, where his big break came in 1961 during a fill-in appearance at the Playboy Club. Gregory's performance won him notice in *Time* magazine and the publicity led to coast-to-coast bookings.

Gregory used his nightclub act to satirize racism and discrimination, and he used his growing visibility, fame, and fortune during the 1960s to support the civil rights movement.

He participated in every major civil rights march and protest during the 1960s and 1970s, including the March on Washington and the Selma March. He endured many arrests and served jail time for protesting racism and participating in demonstrations. In 1965, Gregory was shot while trying to restore peace during the Watts riots.

Two years later, Gregory ran for mayor of Chicago. In 1968, he ran for president on the Freedom and Peace Party ticket. At the time, Gregory had virtually abandoned performing in nightclubs in favor of working the college circuit. In the 1970s, Gregory started using his fame and prominence to influence Black Americans and others to change their diets to become healthier. Gregory died in 2017, on the front line of political causes and human rights issues.

Callie House

1861–1928

FIGHTER FOR EX-SLAVE REPARATIONS

After the Civil War ended and the 13th Amendment was adopted, formally abolishing slavery in the United States, former enslaved African Americans found themselves without resources. To provide relief for former slaves, Callie House, with the assistance of Isaiah Dickerson, chartered the National Ex-Slave Mutual Relief, Bounty and Pension Association in 1898. House, named the secretary of the new organization, eventually became its leader and traveled across the South. One of House's stops was in Boone County, Missouri, where she spent a great deal of time and established a local chapter.

The organization had a dual mission: to petition Congress for the passage of legislation that would grant compensation to ex-slaves, particularly elderly ex-slaves, and to provide mutual aid and burial expenses. Through the use of the mail the organization collected membership fees and monthly dues to help defray lobbying costs, printing and publication expenses, and travel expenses of national officers. Monthly dues were reserved to aid the sick and the disabled and to pay burial expenses. By 1900 the association's nationwide membership was estimated to be around 300,000.

House and her organization faced opposition from both the government and African American leaders. Newspapers of the time often ridiculed House and the association's efforts.

In 1915, the organization filed a class action lawsuit in federal court against the US Treasury for a little over $68 million. The lawsuit claimed that this sum, collected between 1862 and 1868 as a tax on cotton, was due the appellants because the cotton had been produced by them and their ancestors as a result of their "involuntary servitude." The court denied the claim, based on governmental immunity.

Despite the obstacles put before the organization, it continued to flourish until House was imprisoned by the Justice Department on charges of mail fraud, for sending out misleading information. In 1917, after a three-day trial, without definitive evidence, House was sentenced to the Missouri State Prison in Jefferson City. She served the majority of her sentence and was released from prison in August 1918.

House returned to Nashville, the place of her birth, where she died on June 6, 1928, from cancer.

Jefferson Bank Demonstrators

August 30, 1963–March 31, 1964

From August 30, 1963, through March 31, 1964, Jefferson Bank and Trust Company was the scene of a seven-month-long demonstration organized by the St. Louis Chapter of the Congress of Racial Equality (CORE) to force the bank to hire four Black clerical workers. Located in the heart of the Black community, most of the bank's customers were African American but there were no Black employees.

The protest began on August 30, when participants sat down in the lobby and sang, "We shall not be moved." The protests were proceeding despite injunctions obtained by the bank to halt them. A number of organizers were arrested, convicted, and sentenced to fines and jail terms. The demonstrations finally ended when the bank hired five Black clerical employees.

This event marked the beginning of the civil rights movement in St. Louis and led to major changes in hiring practices in the city. From the ranks of the protesters rose many political leaders, including William Clay Sr., who became the first African American elected to the US House of Representatives from Missouri; Raymond Howard and Louis Ford, who became Missouri legislators; Robert Curtis, who became the first African American to run for governor of Missouri; Marion Oldham, who was appointed to the Board of Curators of the University of Missouri;

and Norman Seay, who became an equal opportunity specialist with the US Department of Health, Education and Welfare in Rockville, Maryland.

eon M. Jordan

1905–1970

TEACHER, POLICE DETECTIVE, POLITICIAN, AND BUSINESSMAN

eon Jordan was one of the most influential African Americans in Kansas City history and one of the most powerful Black politicians in Missouri. Born in 1905 in Kansas City, Missouri, Jordan attended Lincoln High School and graduated from Wilberforce University in Wilberforce, Ohio, in 1932. After graduation, he worked as a schoolteacher and social worker.

In 1938, Jordan joined the Kansas City Police Department. The first African American in the department's history, he became a detective and rose to the rank of lieutenant. In 1947, Jordan took a leave of absence and lived eight years in Liberia in West Africa, where he reorganized a 450-man police force. In 1948, Liberian President William Tubman awarded Jordan the Chevalier of the Star of Africa for his help coordinating the rescue of the French High Commissioner of West Africa along with sixteen other French officials after their plane made an emergency landing.

After he returned to Kansas City, Jordan left the police department and launched both his political and business careers. In 1958, Jordan became a Democratic Party committeeman in the Kansas City's 14th ward. In 1963, Jordan and Bruce Watkins, a friend, co-founded Freedom Incorporated, an organization that promoted and advocated political awareness among African Americans in Kansas City through voter registration drives and the development of African American political candidates.

In 1963, the two worked to help pass an accommodation ordinance, desegregating all public facilities in the city. The following year Freedom Incorporated put forward eight candidates for office—and seven won. Jordan was among them, and won his first of three terms in the Missouri House of Representatives.

Jordan was assassinated in a gang-style killing on July 15, 1970, as he was closing his tavern. Charges were brought against two individuals, but no one was convicted. In 2011, forty years after Jordan's death, the *Kansas City Star* reported in a story that the mob boss Nick Civella had signed off on Jordan's killing because he "had angered influential people in the worlds of crime and politics."

A statue of the slain leader, dedicated in 1975, stands in the Leon M. Jordan Memorial Park at 31st Street and Benton Boulevard in Kansas City.

$\mathscr{M}$innie Liddell

1939–2004

DRUM MAJOR FOR EQUAL EDUCATIONAL OPPORTUNITIES

On February 18, 1972, Minnie Liddell filed a class action lawsuit on behalf of her son Craton that would forever change public education in St. Louis. The suit, which led to the most expansive (and maybe one of the most ingenious) school desegregation plans in the nation, consumed almost thirty years of Liddell's life.

All she wanted was for her son to attend his neighborhood school. In the summer before the 1971–72 school year, Liddell was satisfied with nearby Yeatman Elementary School, but the St. Louis Board of Education informed her that the school was overcrowded and her son would be bused to a deteriorating neighborhood some distance away.

Liddell was frustrated because her children were constantly being forced to switch schools and be bused across town. Craton had attended four schools in seven years. Although the suit was filed in 1972, it did not go to trial until 1977, when a judge ruled against Liddell and other parents. A federal appeals court panel reversed the order in 1980, which led to a massive desegregation plan that called for a city- and county-wide transfer program.

The full transfer program began in the fall of 1983, with Black school children rising before dawn to stand on street corners and wait for the long bus ride to a promise of better educational opportunities. Suburban schools that had been predominately white before the program accepted transfer students. The Voluntary

Minnie Liddell, photo courtesy of Mercantile Library at UMSL

Interdistrict Transfer Program succeeded in desegregating classrooms in the city and surrounding suburbs. Fifty-nine percent of the city's African American students were in desegregated schools in 1995, compared to only 18 percent in 1980.

There were mixed reviews regarding academic results of the transfers, showing little academic advancements in the elementary schools but steady gains in the high schools in math and reading. Magnet and transfer students graduated at twice the rate of other city students.

The case was officially closed by a federal judge in 1999, nearly twenty-seven years after it was filed. Craton Liddell died in 2002 and Minnie Liddell died two years later. When she died, the school district held a memorial service at what is now Yeatman-Liddell Middle School, the same school where Craton had been denied admission. On May 11, 2002, the school district dedicated the Minnie Liddell Park next to their central office in downtown St. Louis.

$\mathcal{T}$heodore McMillian

1919–2006
JUDGE

$\mathcal{T}$heodore McMillian, the grandson of slaves, broke down racial barriers and achieved many firsts in the legal profession. Born on January 28, 1919, McMillian attended the St. Louis Public Schools and graduated first in his class from Vashon High School. He attended the old Stowe Teachers College and later Lincoln University in Jefferson City, majoring in physics and mathematics. He wanted to be a physicist but before he could earn enough money to pay for his master's degree, he was drafted into the army.

After his discharge, McMillian decided to enter law school, figuring he was too old to pursue a career in science. He enrolled as the first African American in Saint Louis University Law School and graduated in 1949, at the top of his class. He was the first African American named to Alpha Sigma Nu, the national Jesuit honor society. After graduation, McMillian launched his career at the law firm of Alphonse J. Lynch, where he took on a successful case against the city of Webster Groves, Missouri, for the integration of the city's swimming pool.

McMillian went on to become the first African American assistant prosecutor in the city of St. Louis. In 1956, Governor Phil M. Donnelly appointed him St. Louis circuit court judge, the first African American circuit court judge in Missouri. McMillian later became the first Black member of the Missouri Court of

CITY OF WEBSTER GROVES SWIMMING POOL.
PHOTOS COURTESY OF MERCANTILE LIBRARY
AT UMSL

Appeals, Eastern District and the first African American to reach the 8th US Circuit Court of Appeals.

McMillian was dedicated to the St. Louis community and worked hard to improve the lives of its citizens. He was one of the founders of the Herbert Hoover Boys and Girls Club and one of the founders of the Human Development Corporation, an anti-poverty agency. He also founded what is now Legal Services of Eastern Missouri. Late in his life, McMillian donated a quarter of a million dollars to Saint Louis University Law School to assist students in need of financial aid.

When McMillian died in 2006, he left behind written landmark decisions on desegregation, free speech, civil rights, employment discrimination, and affirmative action.

$\mathcal{T}$heodore D. McNeal

1905–1982
POLITICIAN AND ORGANIZER

$\mathcal{M}$issouri's first African American state sena-
tor and a union organizer for the Sleeping Car
Porters, Theodore McNeal was born in Helena,
Arkansas, on November 5, 1905. He attended the local public
schools and after graduation from high school moved to St. Lou-
is, where he obtained employment in a ceramic and brick plant.
While on vacation in 1930, McNeal took a temporary job as a
Pullman porter.

He became one of the first workers to join the International
Brotherhood of Sleeping Car Porters and soon took on a leadership
role. McNeal was one of the union officials who succeeded in
getting signed a hard-earned contract between the Pullman
Company and the brotherhood, which notably was an agreement
between a large American company and a predominantly Black
union. Later, McNeal became a part of the union's national staff.
He served as a field representative, a primary negotiator, and
eventually as a national vice president.

During World War II, McNeal began promoting fair
employment practices for African Americans in St. Louis, where
he earned a reputation as a civil rights leader. In 1960, McNeal
challenged incumbent Senator Edward J. "Jellyroll" Hogan for
his 7th District seat. McNeal won the Democratic primary by a
six-to-one ratio, becoming the first African American elected to
the Missouri Senate.

T.D. McNeal discussing the 1940s March on Washington, photo courtesy of Mercantile Library at UMSL

During his ten-year tenure in the senate, McNeal led the passage of the Fair Employment Practices Act (1961), supported the creation of the University of Missouri–St. Louis (1963), and assisted in the passage of the State Civil Rights Code (1965). McNeal resigned from the senate in 1970 and accepted an appointment from Missouri Governor Warren Hearnes to the University of Missouri's governing board, becoming its first African American member. He resigned in 1973 to become president of the St. Louis Board of Police Commissioners, the first African American member.

In recognition of his outstanding contributions to the community, McNeal received numerous awards and recognitions that included honorary degrees from the University of Missouri, Lincoln University, and Lindenwood University. He died on October 25, 1982, following a lengthy illness.

Annie Malone

1869–1957

BUSINESSWOMAN, COSMETOLOGIST, ENTREPRENEUR, INVENTOR, AND PHILANTHROPIST

Annie Malone developed the line of Poro beauty products and founded the associated Poro College, a prominent commercial and educational enterprise promoting cosmetics for African American women. She was born in Metropolis, Illinois, the eleventh of twelve children born to Robert and Isabella Turnbo, who were poor farmers. Both parents died while Malone was still very young, so she went to live with an older sister in Peoria, Illinois.

There, Malone took an interest in hair texture, and in the 1890s she started looking for a better hair treatment for African American women. She discovered that many women were using a variety of procedures to straighten their hair, which was causing scalp and hair damage.

By the early 1900s, Malone had patented the first hot comb and developed a variety of improved ways to treat hair. In 1902, she moved to St. Louis, where she and her assistants began selling her products door to door. In 1917, Malone founded Poro College, a large complex in the Ville neighborhood of St. Louis that boasted an auditorium, theater, classrooms, gymnasium, chapel, dining facilities, and roof garden. The college was the first center in America dedicated to the study and teaching of Black cosmetology.

By 1926, the college employed 175 people locally and had franchised outlets in North and South America, the Philippines, the Caribbean, and Africa. Some 75,000 people were employed

at the branches. Malone became very wealthy. Some reports say her net worth in the 1920s was around $14 million. However, she gave much of her fortune to help other African Americans, donating $25,000 to help build the St. Louis Colored YWCA and giving $10,000 for the construction of the St. Louis Colored Orphan's Home, now known as the Annie Malone Family and Children's Center.

In 1930, during the Great Depression, Malone moved her headquarters to Chicago after suffering financially from her second divorce and two civil lawsuits. Her business never recovered. Malone died of a stroke on May 10, 1957, in Chicago.

$\mathcal{M}$artin L. Mathews

1925–

HUMANITARIAN AND CO-FOUNDER OF MATHEWS-DICKEY
BOYS' AND GIRLS' CLUB

$\mathcal{M}$artin l. Mathews is the recipient of countless awards, including honorary doctorates from Saint Louis University, University of Missouri–St. Louis, and Webster University; and the 1982 US Presidential Citizens Award for lifetime achievement from President Ronald Reagan.

Mathews was born in Neelyville, Missouri, on February 17, 1925, to Mr. and Mrs. Ned Mathews. The family moved to Poplar Bluff, Missouri, where Mathews attended school and met his wife, the late Barbara Albright. Mathews later moved to St. Louis, where he was employed with the Burkart Randall Division of Textron, Inc., and later promoted manager of the upholstery department.

Mathews found his calling with community service. He has dedicated over forty-eight years in service to the community. In 1960, he and the late Hubert "Dickey" Ballentine co-founded the Mathews-Dickey Boys' Club (in 2001, it became the Mathews-Dickey Boys' and Girls' Club) under a shade tree in St. Louis's W. C. Handy Park. Mathews retired in 2014 after many years as the president and CEO of the club, which serves more than 40,000 young men and women annually from the St. Louis metropolitan area.

Mathews has been involved with the club at both the macro and micro level. He coached the Mathews-Dickey Knights, leading his team of thirty young men to victories on the baseball field

with skills they transferred to the classroom and community. Thousands of successful alumni have graduated from the program and are making their mark in the community. Over the years, Mathews has forged relationships with the business community, and community leaders and the club have successfully raised millions of dollars for programs and facility construction.

Mathews's efforts have garnered national attention, beginning in 1982 when President Reagan declared the club a model for the country. Other national highlights included recognition on NBC's *Today Show* and being featured in Anheuser-Busch's nationally aired commercial, which promoted the club's "Three R" concept—respect, restraint, and responsibility. Vice President Dan Quayle and Supreme Court Justice Clarence Thomas paid a visit to the club, and the White House declared Mathews-Dickey a 21st Century Community Learning Center.

In addition, Mathews is the founder of the Earn and Learn Program, a training effort that enables young people to earn money as managers, coaches, scorekeepers, and umpires. He has dedicated countless hours serving on educational boards and corporate committees whose aim is to improve the quality of life in the community.

$\mathcal{I}$vory Perry

1930–1989
CIVIL RIGHTS ACTIVIST

$\mathcal{I}$vory Perry was one of the faithful participants in the St. Louis civil rights movement from the 1960s to the 1980s and drew the city's attention to the threat of lead poisoning through environmental racism.

Born in rural Arkansas in 1930, Perry was the son of sharecropper parents and never had the benefit of a formal education. He joined the US army in 1948 and served in one of the last segregated units during the Korean War. After he was discharged, Perry came to St. Louis in 1954. He became involved with the civil rights movement within a few years.

Perry organized rent strikes, laid down in front of cars, chained himself to factory fences in support of striking workers, and staged sit-ins at the mayor's office. He was often arrested in the process. When the Jefferson Bank demonstrations for equal employment began, Perry could always be depended upon to be on the picket line.

During the 1960s, Perry worked for the Human Development Corporation as a field housing specialist, where he found a type of racial injustice other than segregated lunch counters or the exclusion of Blacks from jobs or voting. He found Blacks crowded into substandard housing, and he began organizing for tenant rights and the rent strike of 1969. While visiting renters in their homes, Perry noticed recurring health problems among children and found those problems could be traced to lead-based paint.

Perry began an intensive campaign to eliminate the threat of lead poisoning in the lives of St. Louis's inner-city tenants. His desire was to get legislation passed that would force landlords to remove lead-based paints from their buildings. Although Missouri had outlawed the use of lead-based paints in buildings in 1950, some paint still remained on the walls and woodwork of many older buildings. Perry was especially concerned because many of the victims were small children, and daily contact with lead-based paint could result in brain damage and mental retardation.

In 1970, with the help of an alderman, Perry got an ordinance passed that forced landlords to remove lead-based paint from their properties. When judges and municipal authorities failed to actively enforce the law, Perry began an educational and lead-testing campaign to help save countless children.

On February 16, 1989, Perry was stabbed to death by his son during a domestic quarrel.

$\mathcal{J}$ohn Edward Perry

1870–1962
PHYSICIAN

$\mathcal{J}$ohn Edward Perry, the founder of Wheatley-Provident Hospital in Kansas City, Missouri, arrived in Kansas City in 1903 with his medical bag and a dream to build an African American–owned hospital. The son of parents who were formerly enslaved, Perry was born in Clarksville, Texas, in 1870. He graduated from Bishop College in Marshall, Texas, and received his MD degree from Meharry Medical College in Nashville.

After graduation, Perry came to Missouri. He first stopped in Joplin but stayed only one day due to the limited number of African Americans there. Next he traveled to Jefferson City, where he took the state medical examination. Perry was advised not to establish a practice in that city. Determined to remain in the state, Perry went to Mexico, Missouri, where he received a warm welcome from two white physicians. One shared the following motto, which Perry took on as his code for life: "It is never too cold, the snow is never too deep, the heat never too severe for me to get to the aid of a fellow physician be he white as snow or as Black as tar."

In Mexico, Perry found himself in need of additional training. After six months he moved to Columbia, which had a large African American population. He worked there for a couple of years with a goal of returning to school. He enrolled in the Chicago Post-Graduate Medical School by mail, only to be told when he

arrived that he was not welcome because of his race. He remained, because by law the school could not deny him admission.

It was at this point that Perry decided that a hospital had to be built where African American physicians could practice and learn. After six months, Perry returned to Columbia but was drafted into the Spanish-American War. After the war he returned to Kansas City, where in 1910 he established the fifteen-bed Perry Sanitarium, later renamed Wheatley-Provident Hospital. Perry continued to push for a larger facility and eventually bought property for the Wheatley Hospital in 1916. Perry served as the first superintendent, a position he held for twenty years.

Perry retired from practice in 1945 after fifty years of service. He later traveled to Houston, Texas, to serve as a consultant to a new hospital for African Americans. He returned to Kansas City, where he worked until his death in 1962.

President John F. Kennedy said of Perry: "A Negro American who despite the handicaps of race and poverty lifted himself by his own bootstraps to respected prominence in the medical profession, and American civilization."

$\mathcal{H}$omer G. Phillips

1880–1931

ATTORNEY AND CRUSADER WITH A MISSION

At the corner of Whittier and Kennerly avenues in St. Louis stands a monument to Homer Gilliam Phillips, the namesake of Homer G. Phillips Hospital, which opened in 1937 to serve the city's African American population and provide a place for Black professionals to practice and develop their skills. The building is now a senior community.

In 1922, Phillips lent his considerable support to an $87 million city bond issue with the understanding that $1 million would be used to build a new city hospital for the Black community. Attempts were made to break that promise and use the funds to build a "colored" annex to City Hospital on the south side. Efforts also were made to have African Americans use the outdated Deaconess Hospital. Phillips led the fight that eventually persuaded city leaders to build a new, fully-funded hospital.

Phillips never lived to see the hospital that was built in his honor. He was murdered on June 18, 1931. On that day, he left his home at 1121 Aubert Avenue and began walking to the corner of Aubert Avenue and Delmar Boulevard, where he leaned up against a building reading a newspaper while waiting for the streetcar that would take him to his office. Two men approached Phillips. One hit him in the face, drew an automatic pistol, and fired several shots into Phillips. The two men fled into an alley. Later, two men were captured and indicted, but were released due to a lack of evidence. To date no motive has

been determined and no one has been convicted of the murder.

Born in 1880 in Sedalia, Missouri, Homer G. Phillips was orphaned at an early age and raised by an aunt. Phillips's interest in law took him to Washington, D.C., where he lived with African American poet Paul Lawrence Dunbar while attending Howard University Law School. He also worked briefly in the US Justice Department. After graduation Phillips returned to Missouri, where he married and established a law practice and became powerful in Republican politics. Phillips remained a maverick, someone willing to speak out when he felt things were wrong.

$\mathcal{W}$endell Oliver Pruitt

1920–1945
TUSKEGEE AIRMAN

$\mathcal{A}$s a Tuskegee Airman, Wendell Oliver Pruitt flew seventy combat missions overseas and is credited with disabling a German destroyer, shooting down three enemy planes in the air, and destroying several other planes on the ground. For his skill and courage in combat, he was decorated with the Distinguished Flying Cross and Air Medal with four oak leaf clusters.

Because of his outstanding performance in the military, St. Louis proclaimed December 12, 1944, as Captain Wendell O. Pruitt Day. When Pruitt was honored at City Hall, he said, "My highest hope and the highest hope for other (Black soldiers) is that we will find the Four Freedoms realized here when we return."

On April 15, 1945, just five months after the celebration, Pruitt and a student pilot were killed in a plane crash during a training exercise.

Pruitt grew up in St. Louis, the youngest of ten children born to Elijah and Melanie Pruitt. After graduating from Sumner High School, he briefly attended Stowe Teachers College, and later transferred to Lincoln University in Jefferson City, where he obtained civilian pilot training. While in Jefferson City, Pruitt received his private pilot license from the Jefferson City Airport.

After Pruitt graduated from Lincoln in 1941, he was accepted into the US Army Air Corps Flying School at Tuskegee, Alabama. Upon completion of the pre-flight training and gunnery school

and the primary, basic, and advanced flight training, Pruitt was commissioned second lieutenant in December 1942 and assigned to the 302nd Fighter Group.

After his death, Pruitt was honored in 1952 when St. Louis named a federally subsidized high-rise housing project after him. Pruitt-Igoe originally was segregated, with the Pruitt apartments set aside for African Americans and the Igoe apartments for white residents. Unending problems at the complex caused it to be demolished in 1972. In 1984, the St. Louis Board of Education established the Pruitt Military Academy. Also, American Veterans (AMVETS) posts in Michigan and Missouri were named in honor of Pruitt.

$\mathcal{V}$incent E. Reed

1928–2017
EDUCATOR

$\mathcal{V}$incent E. Reed maintained a long and distinguished career. He served as vice president for communications for the *Washington Post*, assistant secretary for Elementary and Secondary Education for the US Department of Education, and superintendent of public schools in Washington, D.C.

The fourteenth of seventeen children, Reed was born in St. Louis on March 1, 1928, to Velma and Artie D. Reed. He attended the St. Louis Public Schools and graduated from Sumner High School. He continued his education with a bachelor of science degree from West Virginia State University, master in education degree from Howard University, and postgraduate studies at the University of Pennsylvania's Wharton School of Business.

After serving in the Korean War, Reed enrolled at West Virginia State College to study printing and coaching and later operated a printing business. In 1956, he joined the D.C. public school system as a teacher and rose through the ranks to superintendent of schools, a role from which he retired. Reed as superintendent was responsible for the daily operation of the D.C. schools, which included 18,000 employees, 7,600 of which were teachers, and approximately 150,000 students.

In 1981, Reed was appointed assistant secretary of Elementary and Secondary Education by President Ronald Reagan, where he was able to continue his passion for education and children. In this position Reed managed over thirty-eight separate programs and

PHOTO COURTESY OF VINCENT E. REED

administrated an annual budget of over $5 billion in the 16,000 school districts across the United States. Reed also represented the administration before Congress regarding federal legislation on appropriations actions and carried out special assignments given by the president of the United States and the secretary of the Department of Education. In March 1982, Reed joined the *Washington Post* as vice president for communications, with the responsibility of chairing the *Post*'s charitable contributions committee and overseeing the *Post*'s support and involvement in charitable and community events, educational programs, and the matching gifts program. During his time at the *Washington Post*, Reed made countless speeches to a wide array of audiences representing the paper.

Reed's deeds have not gone unrecognized. He served on various institutions' boards of trustees and held a number of honorary degrees. He died in 2017 in Washington, D.C. where he lived with his wife Frances Bullitt Reed.

oscoe Robinson Jr.

1928–1993
FOUR-STAR ARMY GENERAL

America's first African American four-star general, Roscoe Robinson Jr., was born in St. Louis on October 11, 1928. He attended St. Louis Public Schools and graduated from Sumner High School. After graduation, he attended Saint Louis University for one year and then transferred to the US Military Academy at West Point, where he received a bachelor's degree in military engineering in 1951. He later attended the US Army Command and General Staff College and the University of Pittsburgh in 1964, where he received a master's degree in international affairs.

For his exceptional courage in the battle for Pork Chop Hill during the Korean War, Lieutenant Robinson earned the Bronze Star. He was then selected as a member of the staff of the US military mission to Liberia in the late 1950s. Robinson was later chosen to command the 2nd Battalion, 7th Calvary, 1st Air Division in Vietnam, and it was during this time that he led a hugely successful joint forces incursion westward into Cambodia. Later that year, Robinson led the 7th Cavalry in another attack in the same area, which caused massive losses to the North Vietnamese. For his heroic and outstanding service in Vietnam, Robinson received the Legion of Merit, the Distinguished Flying Cross, eleven Air Medals, and the Silver Star.

After Vietnam, Robinson served as the executive officer to the chief of staff at the National War College for three years. He

was later promoted to brigadier general and in 1975 became commanding general of the United States Garrison, Okinawa. In 1976, Robinson commanded America's Guard of Honor, the 82nd Airborne Division, as a major general at Fort Bragg, North Carolina. His final military assignment was as US military representative to the North Atlantic Treaty Organization (NATO) Military Committee from 1982 to 1985. After his retirement in 1985, Robinson was awarded by the US Secretary of Defense with the Defense Distinguished Service Medal and a second distinguished service medal.

Robinson then served on various corporate boards, including those of McDonnell-Douglas Corporation and Northwest Airlines. He also was instrumental in the development of the minority studies program at West Point. In May 1993, he received the Distinguished Graduate Award from the West Point Association of Graduates.

Robinson died in 1993 of leukemia and is buried in Arlington National Cemetery. In 2000, West Point named an auditorium in his honor.

$\mathcal{S}$helley Family

1948

SHELLEY V. KRAEMER COURT DECISION

$\mathcal{O}$n May 3, 1948, the US Supreme Court in a unanimous decision handed down the landmark Shelley v. Kraemer decision, which had a profound impact on housing in America. The decision proclaimed race restrictions in housing to be a violation of the 14th Amendment of the US Constitution and impacted over one thousand blocks in the St. Louis area and 20 million other Americans.

The individuals behind the case and the headlines were J. D. and Ethel Shelley. Both were born in Starksville, Mississippi, J. D. in 1905 and Ethel in 1907. They married with their parents' consent when J. D. was eighteen and Ethel sixteen. During the next thirteen years they had five children. After J. D. assisted a woman who had been severely beaten after wrongly being accused of stealing a watch, he felt he had to leave Starksville for his own safety.

J. D. arrived in St. Louis in 1939. He found a house to rent and sent for Ethel and the children. The couple found employment and began saving money to purchase their own home. With the assistance of their pastor and a white realtor, the Shelleys found a home at 4600 Labadie Avenue for sale for $5,700. They put six hundred dollars down. Shortly after moving in, the Shelleys were served with a summons to appear in court to show cause why they should not be prevented from purchasing the new house.

ATTORNEY GEORGE VAUGHN, PHOTOS COURTESY OF JOHN A. WRIGHT SR.

The Shelleys were unaware that the house was under a restrictive covenant that barred "people of the Negro or Mongolian Race" from occupying the property. Louis Kraemer, who lived ten blocks away, had sued to stop the Shelleys from taking possession of the property. The case opened on October 9, 1945, in St. Louis Circuit Court, with Attorney George Vaughn representing the Shelleys. After hearing the arguments the judge ruled in the Shelleys' favor. Kraemer and his attorney appealed to the Missouri Supreme Court, where the lower court decision was reversed in favor of Kraemer. The Shelleys were ordered to repay the $70.01 in court costs to Kraemer. With the assistance of the Real Estate Brokers Association, attorney Vaughn and the Shelleys then appealed to the US Supreme Court—and won.

David Steward

1951–
BUSINESS EXECUTIVE

*D*avid Steward is the founder and chairman of World Wide Technology, Inc., one of the largest African American owned businesses in America. Steward was born in Chicago in 1951 to Harold Steward, a mechanic, and Dorothy Steward, a homemaker.

The family moved to Clinton, Missouri, where life was not easy. The family was poor, and young Steward faced discrimination and was forced to attend a separate school. He was restricted to sitting in the balcony of the movie theater, and he was not allowed to swim in the community pool. One day, Steward and a small group of African Americans decided to swim in the pool, and did so without an incident. Steward felt his time in Clinton taught him how to persevere and deal with hardship, and taught him not to back down when he was right.

After high school, Steward enrolled in Central Missouri State University, where he graduated with a bachelor's degree in business in 1973. He worked for Wagner Electric as a production manager (1974–76), Missouri Pacific Railroad as a sales representative (1975–79), and Federal Express as a senior accountant (1979–84). While at Federal Express, Steward was recognized as salesman of the year and inducted into the company's Hall of Fame in 1981. Next, Steward owned and operated Transportation Business Specialists and Transportation Administrative Services.

In 1990, Steward co-founded World Wide Technology,

World Wide Technology, Inc.

Inc., which provides technology products, services, and supply chain solutions to customers around the globe. From humble beginnings, the company has grown into one of the largest Black-owned companies in the United States, with more than $4 billion in annual revenue and 1,800 employees. Steward gives back to the community. He co-chaired the search committee for a new CEO for the United Way of Greater St. Louis, donated $1 million to the US Army for its museum, is a member of the University of Missouri's board of curators and assisted the university in joining the Southeastern Conference, which provides greater access to athletic competition.

Steward has received numerous awards, including the Lifetime Achievement Award from the Urban League of Metropolitan St. Louis, honorary doctorates from Harris-Stowe State University and Lindenwood University, and other honors that recognize him among the top entrepreneurs and business leaders in the nation.

Clarence Thomas

1948–

US Supreme Court Associate Justice

In 1991, President George H.W. Bush selected Clarence Thomas to replace retiring Supreme Court Justice Thurgood Marshall, the first African American to serve on the court. Thomas's confirmation hearing was far from easy— he faced accusations of inappropriate behavior from Anita Hill, who worked for Thomas at the Department of Education and subsequently at the Equal Employment Opportunity Commission. Thomas denied the accusations and was confirmed.

Since coming on the Court, Thomas is generally has been viewed as among the most conservative members. He has stated that he takes positions that he believes uphold the original meaning of the US Constitution.

Thomas was born in Pinpoint, Georgia, on June 23, 1948. His father left when Thomas was very young, and he and his sister were sent to live with his grandparents. As a child, Thomas knew what it was to be poor and in need, which may have been one of the driving forces for his early career choice.

As a young man, Thomas wanted to become a Catholic priest. With his grandfather's encouragement, Thomas attended and graduated from St. John Vianney Minor Seminary in 1967. After graduation he enrolled in Immaculate Conception Seminary in Conception, Missouri. He left the seminary in 1968, after hearing a fellow student make fun of the death of Dr. Martin Luther King. Thomas headed north and enrolled in Holy Cross College in

US SUPREME COURT, PHOTOS COURTESY OF US SUPREME COURT

Massachusetts. During his time there, Thomas became involved in the establishment of the Black Student Union, the struggle for civil rights, and protests against the Vietnam War. After graduation Thomas enrolled in Yale University Law School.

After receiving his law degree, Thomas came to Missouri, where he worked for several years as an assistant to Missouri Attorney General John Danforth. He later worked as an attorney for Monsanto Company in St. Louis. In 1981, Thomas moved to Washington, D.C., where he received two presidential appointments from President Ronald Reagan: assistant secretary for Civil Rights at the US Department of Education in 1981 and chairman of the Equal Employment Opportunity Commission (EEOC) in 1982. In 1990, President George H. W. Bush gave Thomas his first and only judgeship when he nominated him to the US Circuit Court of Appeals.

Charles Henry Turner

1867–1923

TEACHER AND ENTOMOLOGIST

Charles Henry Turner was an internationally acclaimed entomologist recognized for his research and contributions to the study of small insects. That research laid the foundation for the study of animal behavior psychology during the first two decades of the twentieth century.

Through his research, Turner was able to prove that insects could hear and distinguish pitch, and honeybees could distinguish color and were drawn to flowers by sight and odor. He also found that the common cockroach learned by trial and error and wasps used visual landmarks to find their way back to their colony. Turner was elected to the St. Louis State Academy of Sciences and was made an honorary member of the Illinois State Academy of Science and the Entomological Society of America.

Turner was born in Cincinnati in 1867, the son of Thomas and Addie Campbell Turner. Both of his parents had a strong love for learning and they shared that love with their son, who was exposed to the family library of hundreds of books. Turner attended the local elementary school and Gaines High School, the first high school for African Americans in Ohio, where he graduated as class valedictorian.

In 1891, Turner earned a bachelor's degree, and he received a master's degree in biology one year later from the University of Cincinnati, the first African American to earn a graduate degree from the university. He was awarded a PhD, summa cum laude,

in zoology from the University of Chicago in 1907. Turner's first teaching assignment was as professor of biology at Clark College in Atlanta. He later worked in Georgia, Tennessee, and Indiana in several positions that ranged from classroom teacher to principal to college professor.

In 1908, Turner and his family moved to St. Louis when he accepted a position at Sumner High School. Despite offers to do research full time at prestigious institutions, Turner remained at Sumner until illness forced him to retire in 1922. He died in 1923 in Chicago.

After Turner's death, the St. Louis Board of Education named a new facility for physically disabled children the Charles H. Turner School (pictured here). In 1954, the school became Turner Middle School, which closed in 2010.

$\mathcal{M}$adame C. J. Walker

1867–1919

BUSINESSWOMAN AND HUMANITARIAN

$\mathcal{S}$arah Breedlove McWilliams Walker, a pioneer Black businesswoman and millionaire, was known as Madame C. J. Walker. Born to formerly enslaved parents on a cotton plantation near Delta, Louisiana, in 1867, Walker lost her parents to yellow fever in 1874. To survive, she and an older sister went to work in the cotton fields near Vicksburg, Mississippi. At age fourteen, Walker married Moses McWilliams. Six years later she was a widow with a small daughter to support.

In 1887, Walker moved to St. Louis, where she remained for eighteen years working as a washerwoman for $1.50 a day. During this period, her hair began to fall out. She tried various remedies, but nothing seemed to help. Then, one night in a dream, Walker watched as an old man showed her a mixture to use for her hair.

When she awoke, Walker combined the soaps and ointments in washtubs to create what became known as the "Walker Method." She tried the new formula on herself and friends, realized its potential, and decided to market it. Walker knew the value of marketing, as she had worked for Annie Turnbo Pope Malone's Poro Company, selling Poro's Wonderful Hair Grower.

In 1905, Walker and her daughter, A'Lelia, moved to Denver with $1.50 in savings. There, she re-married, to a newspaper sales agent named Charles Joseph Walker. With his assistance, Walker

established a hair care business. She traveled widely to demonstrate her products, and in 1908, she opened a second office in Pittsburgh. In 1910, she consolidated her enterprises in Indianapolis and founded the Madame C. J. Walker Manufacturing Company.

Always concerned about the Black community, Walker generously contributed to the Tuskegee Institute, the National Association for the Advancement of Colored People (NAACP), and to Black charities in America and abroad. At the time of her death, Walker was the nation's wealthiest African American woman. She owned a mansion in Westchester County, New York, designed by the first registered Black architect, Vertner Tandy. The luxurious home was filled with Aubusson carpets and tapestries and even boasted an Auguste Rodin sculpture.

$\mathcal{M}$axine Waters

1938–
US REPRESENTATIVE

$\mathcal{M}$axine Waters, former chairman of the Congressional Black Caucus, is one of the most powerful Black women in the country to hold elective office. Born Maxine Carr in Kinloch, Missouri, in 1938, she was the fifth of thirteen children born to Remus and Velma (Moore) Carr. Her parents separated while she was very young and she went to work at thirteen as a bus girl in a segregated restaurant. Later, she worked in a factory to help support the family. After graduating from Vashon High School, she married Edward Waters and they had two children: Edward and Karen.

In 1961, the family moved to Los Angeles in search of better employment opportunities. They found only low-paying jobs. The turning point in Waters' life came in 1955, when she discovered Head Start, a federally funded program to help children in low-income families. Waters became an assistant teacher and later a supervisor.

In 1970, Waters began to get involved in local and state political affairs. She became the chief deputy for Los Angeles Councilman David S. Cunningham and she enrolled in California State University in Los Angeles, where she earned a B.A. degree in sociology.

In 1976, Waters was elected to the California State Assembly. She sponsored a bill that was successfully enacted in 1984 that prohibited police from strip-searching people arrested for

US House of Representatives, photo
courtesy of the US Government

misdemeanors not involving weapons, drugs, or violence. One of her greatest achievements was her bill barring California from investing in companies that engaged in trade with South Africa. She also helped to establish the Child Abuse Prevention Training Program, the first of its kind in the United States, and she introduced the nation's first plant closure law.

Waters became the California State Assembly's first female majority leader, the first woman member of the Rules Committee, and the first person without a legal degree to sit on the Judiciary Committee.

In 1990, Waters easily won the seat of US Representative Augustus F. Hawkins, who had retired a year earlier. As a US representative, Waters has obtained assistance for veterans, has become a spokeswoman for the poor and disadvantaged, and has been an outspoken opponent of the Iraq War. She has been honored for her accomplishments often, and her name is on the St. Louis Diamond Walk of Fame in downtown St. Louis.

$\mathcal{H}$enry Wheeler

1886–1964
CIVIL RIGHTS ACTIVIST

$\mathcal{H}$enry Winfield Wheeler, one of St. Louis's early civil rights activists, fought for the rights of all African Americans in St. Louis, but especially for those in the US Postal Service, where he worked for nearly fifty years. Wheeler was born in Jonesboro, Arkansas, in 1886. After graduating from high school in Texarkana, Arkansas, he attended Arkansas State Normal School in Pine Bluff, Arkansas, and graduated in 1908.

Wheeler moved to St. Louis in 1912 and began work as a mail carrier the following year. Tiring of racial insults on his route, he took the clerk's examination and was transferred to that position. Wheeler soon took an active role in the all-Black National Alliance of Postal Employees, which was organized when the Postal Workers refused membership to African Americans. He led demonstrations against segregated Post Office polices and documented four hundred charges of discrimination himself. Wheeler forwarded his complaints to the postmaster general in Washington, D.C., sending copies to President Harry S. Truman. Because of his activism, at one time many whites and Blacks considered Wheeler a troublemaker.

Because of Wheeler's concern for problems brought on by the secondary status given to African Americans in the city, he walked a picket line for seven years in front of the American Theatre until it opened to all on an equal basis in 1955. By then,

USPS HENRY W.
WHEELER STATION,
PHOTO COURTESY
OF JOHN A.
WRIGHT SR.

Wheeler was considered an outstanding leader and was elected a representative to the Missouri Legislature in 1956. To educate the African American community on the history and struggles of African Americans, Wheeler wrote a column for the *St. Louis Argus* newspaper titled "Missing Pages from History."

Wheeler also wrote about well-known African leaders in St. Louis, including John Berry Meachum, James Milton Turner, and Charlton Tandy. Tandy was one of Wheeler's heroes, and after Tandy's death, Wheeler made a decision to continue Tandy's work in the fight for first-class citizenship for African Americans in St. Louis. He did so until his death in 1964. The US Post Office at 12th and Olive now is named for Wheeler.

Ronnie White

1953–

George Draper III

1953–

MISSOURI SUPREME COURT JUDGES AND ATTORNEYS

onnie L. White and George Draper III are the first two African Americans appointed to the Missouri Supreme Court. White was appointed in 1995 by former Governor Mel Carnahan, and Draper was appointed in 2011 by Governor Jeremiah Nixon.

White is a native of St. Louis, born on May 31, 1953. He earned an associate degree from St. Louis Community College, a bachelor's degree from Saint Louis University and a law degree from the University of Missouri–Kansas City. He began his legal career as an intern in the Jackson County prosecutor's office and then served as a legal assistant in the US Department of Defense Mapping Agency.

As an attorney, White worked in the St. Louis Public Defender's Office before opening a private practice. In 1989, he was elected to the Missouri House of Representatives. He resigned in 1992 to become a St. Louis City Counselor. Prior to his appointment to the Missouri Supreme Court, White served as a judge for the Court of Appeals of the State of Missouri for the Eastern Division. White retired from the court in 2007 and again went into private practice. He was recognized for his

accomplishments on the Diamond Walk of Fame in downtown St. Louis.

Draper was born on August 5, 1953, in St. Louis. He attended St. Louis Public Schools until 1964 when his family moved to Silver Springs, Maryland. After high school, he earned a bachelor's degree in psychology from Morehouse College in Atlanta and his juris doctorate from Howard University School of Law in Washington, D.C.

Draper began his legal career in 1981 as a law clerk in the District of Columbia Superior Court. He returned to St. Louis in 1984 and joined the office of the Circuit Attorney of St. Louis. He was promoted to team leader in 1990. Three years later, Draper was appointed first assistant in the Circuit Attorney's Office, a position he held until 1994, when Governor Mel Carnahan appointed him associate circuit judge of the 21st Judicial Circuit in the Civil Division. In 1998, he was appointed circuit judge in the 21st Judicial Circuit and two years later Carnahan appointed him appellate judge in the Missouri Court of Appeals, Eastern Division.

In 2001, Draper participated on the six-member Missouri Appellate Apportionment Commission that handled redistricting, and Draper was retained for twelve years. Later he served as the first African American Chief Judge of the Missouri Court of Appeals, Eastern Division. For his accomplishments, Draper was an inaugural member of the Gallery of the St. Louis Legal Pioneer.

oy Wilkins

1901–1981

CIVIL RIGHTS LEADER

R oy Wilkins was one of the most influential civil rights activists and a steady voice for nonviolence. Wilkins served as the executive director for the National Association for the Advancement of Colored People (NAACP) from 1955 to 1977.

Born in St. Louis, Wilkins moved to St. Paul, Minnesota, as a young child to live with an aunt after his mother died. After graduating from high school, he enrolled at the University of Minnesota. To help pay his tuition, Wilkins worked as a railroad porter, waiter, and a clean-up man in the stockyards. In his spare time he worked as a secretary for the local branch of the NAACP.

After college, Wilkins went to work for the *Kansas City Call*, the city's leading African American newspaper, as managing editor. During Wilkins's time at the paper, he fought hard against the widespread segregation in the town and successfully assisted in the re-election of a anti-segregation senator. Wilkins's efforts brought him to the attention of the NAACP leaders, who offered him the position of assistant executive secretary in 1931. Wilkins served as the editor of *The Crisis*, an NAACP magazine, from 1934 to 1949, after its founder, W. E. B. DuBois, left the organization. In 1955, Wilkins became executive secretary. He remained at the NAACP for forty-six years.

NAACP

Under his leadership the NAACP took legal action to overturn school segregation and encourage civil rights legislation, and membership grew to approximately 500,000. During the civil rights movement, thousands of protesters, including Wilkins, were arrested. The NAACP took the lead by providing bail money along with legal support. Throughout the 1950s and 1960s, the organization played a major role in getting support for the 1964 Civil Rights Act, the 1965 Voting Rights Act, and the 1968 Fair Housing Act. Wilkins was one of the key organizers of the famous March on Washington in 1963, and he earned the nickname "Mr. Civil Rights."

When Wilkins died in 1981, President Ronald Reagan ordered American flags on all government buildings to be flown at half-staff.

$\mathcal{R}$oy Jerome Williams Sr.

1925–2013
PHYSICIAN AND CIVIC RIGHTS ADVOCATE

$\mathcal{R}$oy Jerome Williams Sr. represents the second of three generations of practicing physicians in his family. His father, W. R. Williams Sr., began practicing medicine in St. Louis in 1921, and thirty-four years later the younger Williams followed in his footsteps.

Born in St. Louis in 1925, Williams is a product of the St. Louis Public Schools. After high school graduation he attended Morehouse College and then graduated from Meharry Medical College in Nashville, Tennessee, in 1947. He completed his residency program at Homer G. Phillips Hospital, but illness nearly sidelined his career. In the midst of his training in 1948, Williams became ill with tuberculosis and spent the next two years being treated for the illness. Williams served as head of the tuberculosis service at Homer G. Phillips for two years and then worked as head of the outpatient department for fifteen years. He helped to oversee the building of the hospital's new outpatient clinic.

Williams also has been an active voice against discrimination in education and business. In 1962, he led a march against the St. Louis Board of Education for the desegregation of the public schools, and the following year he was an active participant in the Jefferson Bank demonstration aimed at obtaining employment for African Americans. That event was one of the key events that started the civil rights movement in St. Louis. In 1965, Williams was one of the founders of Gateway National Bank, which was

the only African American bank in Missouri and the eighth institution to be chartered nationwide with substantial Black representation among its founders.

Williams's passion for medicine and serving others has led to a career filled with firsts, including becoming the first African American president of the St. Louis Community College Board of Trustees, the Community College Foundation, and the Missouri State Board of Registration for the Healing Arts. Williams also has served on the Missouri State Board of Education and the St. Louis Board of Police Commissioners along with numerous civic boards and commissions.

For his commitment to the health profession and community service, Williams received numerous awards and honors.

$\mathcal{M}$argaret Bush Wilson

1919–2009
ATTORNEY

$\mathcal{M}$argaret Bush Wilson was the first female African American to head the National Association for the Advancement of Colored People (NAACP) Board of Directors and a civil rights attorney. Born in St. Louis in 1919, she attended public schools. After graduating from Sumner High School, she enrolled at Talladega College in Alabama in 1940 and received a law degree from Lincoln Law School in 1943.

Lincoln was created and opened by the state of Missouri, which chose not to integrate the University of Missouri Law School. Bush was a member of the second class at the school, and one of just two women. She graduated and passed the bar, becoming the second woman of color admitted to practice in the state of Missouri.

After graduation from law school, Wilson became a civil rights lawyer specializing in housing law. She was part of a legal team that challenged a restrictive covenant that barred Black home buyers from certain white-only neighborhoods in Missouri. Wilson was counsel for the Real Estate Brokers Association, which was formed at her father's initiative to take the case of *Shelley v. Kraemer* to court. The case was won in the US Supreme Court, which ruled that restrictive covenants were unenforceable in the courts.

In 1948, Wilson became the first Black woman in Missouri to run for Congress. She ran with the Progressive Party, and lost the race. Wilson later joined the Democratic Party.

Wilson moved quickly through the presidencies of the St. Louis and Missouri chapters of the NAACP in the late 1950s and early 1960s. In 1963, she was elected to the national board and became chairman of the organization in 1975. After a bitter dispute with Benjamin L. Hooks, the organization's executive director, and a disagreement with the board, Wilson was removed from the national board.

Her professional experience included serving as United States Attorney for the Rural Electrification Administration of the US Department of Agriculture and Assistant Attorney General of Missouri. She also served as board chair of her alma mater (Talladega College) and St. Augustine College as well as trustee emerita of Washington University in St. Louis and Webster University, formerly Webster College.

Wilson died in St. Louis in 2009, at the age of ninety, after a forty-year legal career.

$\mathcal{N}$athan B. Young

1896–1993

JUDGE, HISTORIAN, EDITOR, AND ARTIST

*T*hroughout Nathan Young's life, he was a tireless researcher and writer who left a true legacy for future generations. Born in 1896 in Tuskegee, Alabama, Young's father was a professor at Tuskegee Institute. He graduated from Florida Agricultural and Mechanical University, where he played on the baseball and football teams and was in the orchestra. At the urging of a family friend, he enrolled in Yale University Law School and received his law degree in 1918.

After practicing law for a short time in Birmingham, Alabama, Young moved to St. Louis in 1924. He established a law practice, which he maintained until 1958, when he joined the St. Louis City Counselor's Office. He remained there as a prosecutor until 1967, when he was appointed judge of Municipal Court No. 2, a position from which he retired in 1973.

Young was co-founder of and legal counsel for the *St. Louis American* newspaper, which was founded in 1928. The first issue of the *American*, released on March 17, sold out of its two thousand copies with the headline, "Pullman Porters May Strike." The paper was a major supporter of the "Buy where you can work" campaign. At the beginning of the campaign, there were only a few stores with Black clerks. By the end of the campaign, Blacks could be found working in a great number of business establishments. The paper also was a strong supporter of labor organizing among Pullman car porters.

Young also was active in the Harlem Renaissance. His writings appeared in *Opportunity*, published by the National Urban League, and in *The Crisis*, published by the NAACP. Young is remembered by many for his research on African Americans in St. Louis and on Missouri Black folklore. His 1937 publication, *Your St. Louis and Mine*, was one of the first publications to provide histories and photographs of noted Black St. Louisans and Black institutions.

Young's interest in folklore led him to do extensive research on local legends, including "Frankie and Johnny," "Stackolee," the Brady-Duncan Saga, the St. Louis Blues, and Babe Connors. During his later years, Young produced hundreds of paintings, which now are housed at Saint Louis University. He also wrote many essays on local musical legends and others. One on his last publications, "Guest of Honor," was on Scott Joplin.

$\mathcal{J}$ ohn Anderson Lankford

1874–1946
DEAN OF BLACK ARCHITECTS

$\mathcal{J}$ ohn Anderson Lankford was born in Potosi, Missouri, on December 4, 1874, into a poor but well-respected family. His father was a farmer and miner and known for his high integrity and his mother was a devout Christan and temperance worker.

As a youngster, Lankford spent a great deal of his time working in the mines and on the family farm, except when he was in school. After completing school, he went to Crystal City to work in a plate glass factory to earn money to pay his way to Jefferson City, where he was to enter Lincoln Institute, the State College, and the School of Mechanical Arts. After arriving at the school, he soon obtained a job as an assistant janitor, which provided him with enough money to cover his board. To meet his other expenses, he became an agent of the Plymouth Rock Paint Company to earn money to aid him with his clothing needs, and employment as a solicitor with a steam laundry to get his clothes cleaned. At the college, he specialized in mathematics and natural and chemical science. He also finished blacksmithing, carpentry, woodwork, and mechanical drawing.

Once in college, he had little difficulty. He distinguished himself as extraordinary and, at the end of six years, he had finished his course work with an enviable record. With a strong desire to be his own master, he opened a blacksmith shop in St. Louis. For a short period of time, he was superintendent of

the blacksmith department of Fulton Cotton Mill in Atlanta, Georgia. Not being able to take advantage of the knowledge he had learned in college, he decided to look at other fields. He enrolled at Tuskegee Industrial School in Alabama, where he studied two trades along with courses in physics and chemistry and graduated in 1896.

Lankford studied architecture with private architects and later taught architecture and industrial subjects at Tuskegee, A&M University in Normal, Alabama; Shaw University in Raleigh, North Carolina; Wilberforce University in Wilberforce, Ohio; and Edward Waters College in Jacksonville, Florida. Lankford's professional and employment record matched his impressive educational credentials. In 1902 Lankford established L.A. Lankford and Bro., an architectural and builder's office in Washington, D.C., and by 1908 had branch offices in New York; Richmond and Norfolk, Virginia; Baltimore, Maryland; and St. Louis and Kansas City, Missouri.

He designed many buildings, including schools and churches. In World War I he was a construction engineer at the Washington Navy Yard. He also was a consulting architect for the Capital View Realty Company and in the 1930s was the architectural engineer in the Interior Department as a housing consultant.

Lankford organized the local Negro Business League in Washington D.C. in 1908 and was president for three years. He also was president of the National Technical Association and a life member of the National Negro Business League and, in 1907, was elected one of its vice presidents.

Lankford received honorary degrees from Shaw University, Allen University, Wilberforce University, Moris Brown, Atlanta Georgia.

$\mathscr{J}$ordan Chambers

1895–1962

THE NEGRO MAYOR OF ST. LOUIS

hough Jordan Chambers held no official political office as the Black Mayor of St. Louis, he was larger than life, a political power broker whose influence was far-reaching. According to Gwen Moore, curator at the Missouri Historical Society, "Little happened in St. Louis politics or in the Black community in general that Chambers somehow did not have a hand in." The fact that he was able to obtain such power at a time when Blacks in the community had been marginalized is a testament to his political understanding and his human relations skills.

Chambers was born in Nashville, Tennessee, in 1895. He moved to St. Louis with his parents when he was a year old. He attended Sumner High School but left before graduation and obtained a variety of jobs. One was working on the railroad as a cleaner, where he demonstrated his leadership skills when he organized some 1,100 fellow workers into a union to challenge the racial disparity in pay that existed.

His first entrance into politics was in 1925, when he was successful in managing the campaign of Republican mayoral candidate Victor Miller in the Black wards of the city. Later, Chambers, like many other Blacks made a decision to switch from the Republican Party to the Democratic Party to support Franklin Delano Roosevelt. During the 1930s, Jordan led many African American voters out of the Republican party into the Democratic

party. During this period Chambers steadily built a powerful organization that spread from his 19th Ward to most of the city's Black wards. By the 1940s both Black and white political hopefuls at the local and state level were seeking support from Chambers.

Although Chambers was a champion for civil rights, he avoided direct action protests and public demonstrations and opted for leveraging his clout to push for jobs and security for African Americans. It was said that he held meetings or court, as some would say, at his nightclub, Club Riviera, to strategize and forge relationships with leaders of all stripes, including civil rights leaders.

It is reported that Chambers did get involved in a direct protest in the 1940s, the March on Washington Movement (MOWM). He joined civil rights legions like T.D. McNeal and David Grant in the protest against job discrimination in St. Louis by companies with defense contracts.

During Chambers's final illness in 1962, President John Kennedy and Vice President Lyndon Johnson both sent wires expressing their condolences. After he died, more than 2,600 people attended his funeral at St. Paul A.M.E. Church. Three services were held to accommodate the mourners, who ranged from celebrated figures to everyday people whom he assisted during his decades of public service. Missouri Governor John Dalton gave the eulogy. By the time of his death, he had acquired another title, "Father of Black Politics."

Today, Chambers is honored in St. Louis with a United States Post Office and city park bearing his name.

Nathan B. Young

1865–1933
Educator

Nathan Young, an educator who helped advance Black education in the early 20th century, was born in slavery in Newbern, Alabama, on September 15, 1862. Shortly after his birth, he and his mother, Susan Smith, were sold to another plantation owner. She successfully worked out a plot for herself and Nathan to escape slavery to Tuscaloosa. They were successful and ended up in Tennessee, where she married Frank Young. They both wanted Nathan to have an education and enrolled him in a local rural school operated by a white Baptist minister in Tuscaloosa. He later attended Stillman College for three months before enrolling in Talladega College, where he received a classical education in the teacher-training branch.

After Reconstruction, many whites and Blacks agreed that African Americans should limit their education ambitions to training for menial and agricultural labor. Young wanted more for his race and wanted to be instrumental in lifting the "veil of ignorance" from his people. After a brief period of teaching, he decided he wanted to be a better teacher and enrolled in Oberlin College, where he obtained bachelor's and master's degrees.

Soon after graduation from Oberlin, he obtained employment teaching and supervising school programs in the South. Young became a target for white authorities because he advocated for Blacks to be educated the same as whites. They, on the other hand, believed that non-vocational education would be wasted on Blacks.

In 1892, Young was invited by Booker T. Washington, the founder of Tuskegee Institute in Alabama, to serve as head of the academic department of Tuskegee Institute in Alabama. Washington believed that the uplifting of his race meant following the road of vocational education. Young, on the other hand, believed that academics should play a more important role in the advancement of the Black race. After five years, because of their difference in philosophy, Young left Tuskegee for a position at Georgia State Industrial College as the director of teacher training. From there he went on to serve as the president of Florida A&M University.

Young left Florida A&M in 1923 to become president of Lincoln University in Jefferson City, Missouri. He is believed to have been one of the most significant figures in the university's history. He immediately realized little had been done academically to change the school from an institute to a university. One of Young's first tasks was to raise the quality of the university's faculty by attracting individuals with degrees from prestigious northern institutions. Many of these instructors remained at the university for their entire careers. Young also developed plans for the construction of more buildings. Training in Army Reserve Officers' Training Corps (ROTC) also was brought to the university. To keep the public informed throughout the state, Young developed a weekly newsletter.

Young left the university in 1927 due to political pressure and returned two years later. He was removed again in 1931 because of politics. He died on July 19, 1933, leaving a proud legacy and mark at Lincoln University.

"You may encounter defeats,
but you must not be defeated."
—*Maya Angelou*

Performers, Athletes, and Other Notables

"If you have a purpose in
which you can believe, there's
no end to the number of
things you can accomplish."
—*Marion Anderson*

$\mathcal{M}$aya Angelou

1928–2014

POET AND WRITER

$\mathcal{M}$aya Angelou is one of the most accomplished individuals of our time. She has provided a voice for the oppressed for more than five decades through her work as a poet, novelist, educator, dramatist, producer, actress, historian, filmmaker, and civil rights activist.

Angelou was born Marguerite Johnson in St. Louis in 1928, the oldest of two children of Bailey Johnson and Vivian Baxter Johnson. She received the nickname, Maya, which was shortened from "my or mya sister" from her brother, Bailey Jr. Angelou's parents divorced when she was three years old, and she and her brother were sent to live with their grandmother in Stamps, Arkansas. At the age of eight, a crisis occurred early in her life. When she returned to St. Louis to visit her mother, she was raped by her mother's boyfriend. She shared the incident with her brother, and the man was mysteriously murdered. Maya responded by becoming mute, thinking she was responsible for his death, a condition that lasted for almost five years. She returned to live with her grandmother, began to read voraciously and slowly came out of her silence.

After eighth-grade graduation she lived with her mother in San Francisco. One summer she went to visit her father, ran off after they had a quarrel, and lived for awhile with homeless teens in a van. After returning to her mother's home, she got a job as the first African American streetcar conductor in San Francisco.

MAYA ANGELO'S ST. LOUIS CHILD-
HOOD HOME, 3130 HICKORY, PHOTO
BY JOHN A. WRIGHT, SR.

When she turned sixteen, Angelou gave birth to a son and worked a variety of jobs to support the two of them.

In 1952, Angelou married a Greek sailor name Tosh Angelos. The marriage was short-lived, and in 1954 Angelou moved to New York and won a part in the musical *Porgy and Bess*, which toured Africa and Europe. Returning to the United States, she and comedian Godfrey Cambridge wrote a show to raise funds for the civil rights movement. She continued to write and moved to Egypt and Ghana. When she returned to the States in 1966, through the guidance of her friend James Baldwin, she wrote *I Know Why the Caged Bird Sings*, the first of five semi-autobiographical novels.

Angelou remained active until her death in 2014. In recognition of her work, she was awarded the Presidential Medal of Arts, the Lincoln Medal, and three Grammies. President Bill Clinton requested her to compose a poem that she read at his inauguration in 1993.

Henry Armstrong

1912–1988

PRIZE FIGHTER

*H*enry Armstrong—also known as "Hurricane Henry," "The Human Buzzsaw," "Perpetual Motion," "Hammering Hank," and "Homicidal Henry"—was one of the greatest fighters ever and the only fighter to hold three boxing titles simultaneously (featherweight, lightweight, and welterweight) at a time where only eight world titles were recognized.

Born Henry Melody Jackson Jr., Armstrong borrowed a last name from a friend when he began his boxing career. Armstrong fought 181 professional fights and won 152 of them, 100 by knockouts. He also compiled one of the longest winning streaks in boxing, from 1937 to 1939, when he won forty-six straight victories, thirty-nine by knockouts.

Armstrong was born in 1912 in Columbus, Mississippi, to Henry Jackson Sr., a sharecropper of African American, Irish, and Native American descent; and America Jackson, an Iroquois Native American. He was the eleventh of fifteen children. The family moved to St. Louis when he was four years old. As a young child he helped the family by shining shoes to earn money. Armstrong attended the public schools and graduated from Vashon High School just as the Depression was ending.

One day while he was laying tracks for the railroad, a gust of wind blew a newspaper in Armstrong's face, and in it he read an

article about a featherweight boxing champ by the name of Kid Chocolate. When he read that Chocolate had made $75,000 for a thirty-minute fight in New York, reportedly Armstrong said to himself that $75,000 for a half-hour's work had to be better than laying railroad track. He put down his tools and told his friends he was going to be a champion.

After Armstrong retired in 1945, he suffered from alcoholism. He overcame it, became an ordained minister, and served as assistant pastor at First Baptist Church in St. Louis. As director of the Herbert Hoover Boys and Girls Club, he also coached a new generation of boxers. In 1990, he was inducted into the International Boxing Hall of Fame. Armstrong died in Los Angeles in 1988 at the age of seventy-five.

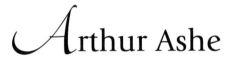

Arthur Ashe

1943–1993
TENNIS CHAMPION

*A*s a child, Arthur Robert Ashe Jr. was not allowed to play on most public tennis courts or to compete in many tournaments because he was an African American—and yet he grew up to become a world-famous tennis champion. Ashe, the son of Arthur Ashe Sr. and Mattie Cunningham Ashe, was born in 1943, in Richmond, Virginia. In 1958, at age fourteen, he reached the semifinals in the under-15 division in the junior national tennis championship, and in 1960 he won the junior singles title.

That same year, Richard Hudlin, a tennis official and Sumner High School teacher in St. Louis, offered Ashe coaching assistance. Ashe moved to St. Louis to live with the Hudlin family. By 1962, he was ranked fifth among US junior tennis players.

After graduation from Sumner, Ashe accepted a tennis scholarship at the University of California at Los Angeles (UCLA). Two years later, he became the first African American male to join the US Davis Cup team. By 1963, Ashe was ranked eighteenth in the senior men's amateur division and had been named to the Davis Cup team. By 1965, he was ranked third and he won the Queensland Championship at Brisbane, Australia. Ashe graduated from UCLA in 1966 with a degree in business administration. He spent six weeks in a Reserve Officers Training Corps program, where he was rated second in his platoon for overall achievement. Ashe ended his military service in 1969

with the rank of first lieutenant. For the next several years, Ashe set winning records in tennis that stood for years.

Ashe was actively involved in the civil rights movement. He was arrested for protesting apartheid in South Africa and the crackdown on Haitian refugees. When Ashe first applied for a visa to enter South Africa in 1970, his request was refused. Three years later, when the country reversed its decision, Ashe became the first African American to play tennis in South Africa's national championships. In 1975, Ashe became the first African American to win the men's singles title at Wimbledon.

After a heart attack in 1979, Ashe underwent quadruple-bypass surgery. He retired the following year with a record of 818 wins and 51 titles. In 1980, Ashe became the first African American captain of the US Davis Cup team, a position he held until 1985. Three years later, when Ashe had to undergo surgery again, a transfusion he received contained blood contaminated with the AIDS virus. In 1993, Ashe died. A statue honoring Ashe, holding books and a tennis racket, stands on Monument Avenue in Richmond.

 rankie Baker

1877–1952
FOLK BALLAD LEGEND

The legendary ballad "Frankie and Johnny" is based on a lover's quarrel that took place on the night of October 15, 1899, when Frankie Baker shot Allen Britt (Johnny) in her apartment at 212 Tree Street in St. Louis.

The two met at a dance at Stolle's Hall at 13th and Biddle streets. Baker, age twenty-two, fell in love with Britt, who was seventeen. She went to great lengths to keep him in money and looking good. The night of the shooting, Baker had gone to the Phoenix Hotel to hear Britt play for a cakewalk. There, she found him in a hallway, kissing eighteen-year-old Alice Pryor.

Baker and Britt quarreled on the street outside the hotel. Baker asked Britt to come home, but he refused. However, around 3:00 a.m., he entered Baker's apartment, where the argument continued. When Britt pulled out a knife and moved toward Baker, she drew a pistol from under her pillow and shot him. He died four days later at City Hospital.

Before twenty-four hours had passed, local songwriter Bill Dooley had composed a ballad that would immortalize the incident and the story. (Later, the title and lyrics were changed from "Frankie and Al" to "Frankie and Johnny.") When Baker stood trial on November 13, 1899, she was acquitted. The killing was deemed a justifiable homicide because Baker had acted in self-defense.

Afterward, people began singing the song whenever they saw Frankie on the street in St. Louis, so she moved to Omaha,

FRANKIE BAKER, PHOTO COURTESY
OF MERCANTILE LIBRARY AT UMSL

Nebraska, to escape the humiliation. When she arrived in Omaha, Baker found the song had got there first, so she moved to Portland, Oregon. There, she worked on the streets and was arrested several times. Around 1925, Baker gave up street life and opened a shoeshine parlor.

In 1935, the movie *She Done Him Wrong* was released, starring Mae West. The story line was altered somewhat, but West did sing the popular ballad. Baker sued Republic Pictures for damages. Unable to convince an all-white jury that Mae West's character was based on her, Baker lost the suit. In 1942, she sued Republic Pictures again when they released the film *Frankie and Johnny*, but she lost again.

Baker was later admitted to a mental hospital in Portland, where she died in 1952. Her story lives on in song.

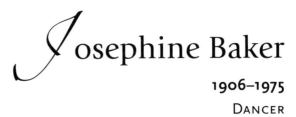Josephine Baker

1906–1975

DANCER

*J*osephine Baker set Paris afire in the 1920s and 1930s with a series of risqué performances. Her dance costumes—including a skirt made from bananas—reportedly were worn to get attention, and Baker did draw plenty of notice. Over the years, Baker grew as a performer, and she remained a major star in the entertainment world for nearly fifty years.

Born in the slums of St. Louis in 1906, Baker entered show business at fourteen, when she abandoned her job as a domestic to enter the world of Black vaudeville. She became a song, dance, and comedy star on the Chitlin' Circuit. Baker first toured with the *Bessie Smith Blues Show* and then became a star in Paris before the age of twenty when she was selected to tour in the all-Black theatrical show *La Revue Negre*. When that show closed, Baker was hired at the *Folies-Bergere*, where she became an instant sensation, drawing international audiences.

After Baker became a French citizen in 1937, she spied on the Italian fascists. During World War II, she worked for the Resistance in North Africa, where she drove an ambulance and entertained the troops. The French government awarded Baker the Croix de Guerre and Legion of Honor. After the war, she adopted four children of different races, a family she called her "Rainbow Tribe." By the 1960s, the tribe had grown to twelve children.

During the late 1940s and 1950s, Baker made several tours

in the United States, where she refused to perform to segregated audiences or stay in segregated hotels. Baker won renewed admiration for speaking out on civil rights. In 1963, she returned to the United States to stand on the podium with Dr. Martin Luther King Jr. at the historic March on Washington.

By 1969, Baker had lost her $2 million home in Paris. When Baker and her children were evicted, Princess Grace of Monaco, a longtime close friend, came to the rescue by giving Baker's family a villa to live in permanently. Baker was far from ready for retirement. Her love for the spotlight and her economic needs drove her to return to the United States to perform at Carnegie Hall in New York. Baker, whose lithe body had not changed since 1925, received a warm welcome from racially mixed audiences.

Baker's life ended suddenly on April 12, 1975, when she succumbed to a heart attack while preparing for her fiftieth anniversary in show business. She was one of the few to be honored with a state funeral in France.

Count Basie

1904–1984
MUSICIAN, BAND LEADER, AND COMPOSER

William "Count" Basie was a prominent Big Band leader during the Swing Era of jazz, an internationally known musician, and a Grammy Award winner. Born on August 24, 1904, in Red Bank, New Jersey, Basie began studying music and playing the piano at an early age under his mother's guidance. He dropped out of school after junior high and was hired at the Palace Theatre in Red Bank to operate the lights and perform music to accompany silent films. As a teenager, Basie also performed wherever he could, mostly at private parties.

In 1924, Basie headed to Harlem, where he hooked up with a vaudeville touring circuit that brought him to major jazz cities such as New Orleans, St. Louis, Chicago, and Kansas City. He got stuck in Kansas City when the Gonzelle vaudeville shows he was traveling with suddenly broke up. Basie played at silent movie theaters for a brief period before joining Walter Page's Blue Devils in 1928 and then the Bennie Moten Band in 1929. Basie remained with the band in Kansas City until Moten's death in 1935.

In 1936, Basie started his own band with some of the best players from Moten's band. The band soon found a steady gig and built up a good reputation at the Reno Club in Kansas City. Soon after, a small Kansas City radio station began carrying the band's live performances from the club. The band then caught the ear of

John Hammond, a wealthy jazz promoter who encouraged them to travel to New York. With Hammond's support, the Count Basie Orchestra made its first recording on the Decca label in 1937.

By the following year, the band was internationally famous, known especially for Basie's unique style of playing and the quality of the musicians and soloists. Basie stuck with the Big Band sound except for a period during the early 1950s when the economy forced him to tour with a septet. For almost fifty years, Basie led bands, and many musicians became prominent through his guidance.

Basie's health began to deteriorate in 1976 after he suffered a heart attack. Following his recovery, he made appearances on stage in an electric wheelchair. Basie died on April 26, 1984, in Hollywood, Florida, of pancreatic cancer. Since his death, Basie has been recognized posthumously with the Presidential Medal of Freedom in 1985, a 32-cent postage stamp with his image by the US Postal Service in 1996, and induction into the New Jersey Hall of Fame in 2009.

Tom Bass

1859–1934

FAMOUS HORSEMAN

*A*t a young age, Tom Bass was known for his skill with animals. During his career, Bass won in competition at every horse show in the country and earned more than two thousand blue ribbons. He also won championships at two World's Fairs, and for many years, he was the only African American to exhibit at the American Royal Horse Shows.

At the height of his career, Bass had gained worldwide recognition. He performed before five US presidents (Coolidge, Cleveland, McKinley, Theodore Roosevelt, and Taft) and he rode in inaugural parades. Bass was honored by Queen Marie of Rumania at the St. Louis Horse Show, rode before royalty, and represented Missouri at the Chicago World's Fair in 1893.

Bass was born into enslavement on January 5, 1859, on the Peter Bass Plantation south of Columbia, Missouri, in Boone County to an enslaved mother, Cornelia Gray, and her owner, William Hayden Bass. The boy grew up on the plantation, which bred and trained horses in addition to raising cattle and crops. Bass was raised by his grandparents, and he learned a great deal from his grandfather, an expert with fine horses.

Shortly after the Civil War, Bass moved to Mexico, Missouri, where he worked as a stable boy and eventually became a trainer well known for his skills and his knowledge of horses. He had a reputation for being gentle and effective, and for having a way with

even the most difficult of horses. After learning the business, Bass opened his own horse-training stable. People from around the country brought their horses to him for breaking in. Though he never became wealthy, Bass was humble and honest, and he was much admired by nearly everyone in the horse show community.

Bass invented the "Bass bit," a bit that prevented the abuse of horses during training. Many of the trophies, cups, and ribbons that Bass won are on display at the American Saddlebred Horse Museum in Mexico, Missouri.

$\mathcal{J}$ames "Cool Papa" Bell

1903–1991
BASEBALL PLAYER

$\mathcal{H}$all of Famer James "Cool Papa" Bell is reported to be the fastest man to have ever played baseball. His teammate Satchel Paige used to say that Bell was so fast, he could turn off the light and be under the covers before the room went dark—but in the re-telling, Paige may have left out the part about faulty electric wiring in the room. That said, Bell was once clocked at circling the bases in 12 seconds, and his prodigious speed allowed him to steal 175 bases in one season, a record.

The legendary player got the name "Cool Papa" for his composure and grace under pressure while playing as a left-handed pitcher with the St. Louis Stars in the early 1920s. After leading the Stars to league titles in 1929, 1930, and 1931 as their center fielder, Bell went on to play with the Detroit Wolves in the East-West League. When the Wolves folded after the Negro League disbanded, Bell moved to Kansas City to play with the Monarchs and at the Mexican Winter Games.

In 1943, Bell signed to play for the Homestead Grays and led them to win the league title in 1942, 1943, and 1944. Two years later, he played for the Detroit Senators, and later he managed the Kansas City Stars.

Bell was born James Thomas Nichols in 1903 in Starkville, Mississippi. He was one of seven children raised by his widowed mother. It is not known when or why he changed his name to

Bell. In 1920, he moved to St. Louis to live with an older brother, to seek employment, and to attend high school.

Though Negro League records are incomplete, Bell's lifetime batting average is ranked tenth on that league's list. He is reported to have batted .400 several times. In 1946, Bell was hitting .411 when he sat out the final doubleheader so that the top batting title could go to another player to help boost him into integrated ball. Although Bell never had a chance to play in the major leagues, he helped others achieve their dreams.

In 1974, Bell was inducted into the National Baseball Hall of Fame, and he is on the St. Louis Walk of Fame. In 1991, Bell died in his home on Dickson Street in St. Louis. Shortly after his death, the city renamed the street James "Cool Papa" Bell Avenue.

Chuck Berry

1926–2017
GUITARIST, SINGER, AND SONGWRITER

Charles Edward Anderson "Chuck" Berry—guitarist, singer, songwriter, and one of the pioneers of Rock 'n Roll—was born in St. Louis on October 18, 1926, the fourth of six children. His parents were Martha and Henry Berry, whose grandparents were enslaved. Berry showed an early talent for music and began singing in the Antioch Baptist Church choir when he was six years old. He gave his first big performance at a talent show at Sumner High School. Although the school administration was said to be disturbed by the performance, it was an enormous hit with the student body.

In 1944, at the age of seventeen, Berry dropped out of high school. He spent three years in the Intermediate Reformatory for Young Men in Jefferson City, Missouri. After his release, Berry returned to St. Louis, got married, and worked for his father in the construction business. He also earned money as a part-time photographer and as a janitor at a local auto assembly plant. Over time, Berry took up the guitar again. In 1951, he began playing in local Black nightclubs with his former classmate Tommy Stevens, who was with the Johnnie Johnson Trio.

Berry's big break came in 1955 when he traveled to Chicago and met with famed blues singer Muddy Waters, who suggested Berry meet with Leonard Chess of Chess Records. A few weeks later, Berry took his song "Maybellene" to the executives at Chess, and they offered him a contract. Within months "Maybellene"

STATUE OF CHUCK BERRY IN UNIVER-
SITY CITY, PHOTO COURTESY OF CURTIS A.
WRIGHT SR.

reached No. 1 on the Rhythm and Blues (R&B) Chart and No. 5 on the Pop Chart. Berry quickly followed with a number of singles, including "Ida Red," which sold over a million copies and reached No. 1 on Billboard's R&B Chart. By the end of the 1950s, Berry was an established star with several hit records, film appearances, and a successful touring career. He also opened a nightclub, now defunct, in St. Louis.

In spite of a number of run-ins with the law, Berry has had a remarkable career. In 1985, he received the Grammy Lifetime Achievement Award, and the following year he was the first inductee in the Rock and Roll Hall of Fame. Berry remains one of the genre's most influential musicians and until his death made regular appearances at concerts and clubs around the country, including Blueberry Hill, located in University City, a suburb of St. Louis. An eight-foot bronze statue honoring Berry stands near the club.

$\mathcal{B}$lind Boone

1864–1927
CONCERT PIANIST

$\mathcal{J}$ohn William "Blind" Boone, a sightless pianist whose musical gifts excited audiences across the United States, Canada, and the British Isles for forty-seven years, was born on May 17, 1864, in a federal camp at Miami, Missouri, in Saline County. At the age of six months, a disease described as "brain fever" struck Boone. In order to save Boone's life, a doctor removed the infant's eyes to relieve pressure on his brain. When Boone was a toddler, his mother moved the family to Warrensburg, Missouri.

Boone's talent for music was noticed early on, after his mother gave him a tin whistle. He quickly mastered the toy. He took up a mouth organ and soon was playing to crowds on the street corners of downtown Warrensburg. In order to help develop Boone's talent, in 1873 some residents of Warrensburg sent him to the Missouri School for the Blind in St. Louis. After he was forced to make brooms rather than develop his musical talents, Boone left the school.

In 1879, John Lange, a respected Black contractor, heard Boone play piano and became his manager. At the age of twenty-one Boone became a full partner with Lange, and they traveled the country. Boone's musical selections, including ragtime compositions of his own, encompassed a wide range of genres, everything from classical music to the touching melodies of plantation songs.

Concert halls and theaters all over the nation clamored for appearances by Boone. He routinely made two or three appearances a day, six days a week, nine months a year. It is estimated that he traveled 300,000 miles throughout North America, plus he made two trips to Europe. Critics not only applauded him for his dynamic musical creativity, but also credited him with introducing Negro spirituals to the concert stage.

Boone closed his final concert season at Virden, Illinois, on May 31, 1927. Although requests for concerts continued to come in, Boone's doctor advised him not to accept. Boone was scheduled to undergo medical treatment at Hot Springs, Arkansas, and he planned a stop in Warrensburg on the way, to visit relatives. On October 4, 1927, Boone collapsed and died on his arrival in Warrensburg.

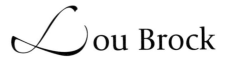

ou Brock

1939–2020
Baseball Player

*H*all of Famer Lou Brock spent the majority of his career as a St. Louis Cardinal. He joined the team in 1964 and played left field. While with the Cardinals, Brock broke Ty Cobb's all-time Major League record for stolen bases. Brock stole 938 bases, and he is ranked 23rd on the all-time hit list with 3,023 lifetime hits. He also was named one of the top 100 players of the twentieth century.

Brock holds the highest batting average record (.391) in twenty-one or more World Series games, and he is the only player in Major League Baseball history to have an award established in his name while still playing. The Lou Brock Award is given each year to the National League Player with the most stolen bases.

Brock was born on June 18, 1939, in El Dorado, Arkansas, to a family of sharecroppers. As a youngster he was a fan of the Brooklyn Dodgers, who had a number of outstanding African American players. Brock grew up in Collinston, Louisiana, on a cotton plantation. He attended Union High School in Mer Rouge, where he played baseball and basketball and was a member of the math and chemistry teams. After high school, he enrolled at Southern University in Baton Rouge, which he attended on an academic scholarship.

When Brock's grades slipped and he lost his scholarship at the end of the first semester, something inside urged him to try out for the baseball team. He did—and he received an athletic scholarship. While at Southern, Brock was selected by the United States Olympic Committee to play on the US Pan American Baseball Team. He also led Southern to the National Association of Intercollegiate Athletics' World Series Championship.

At the end of his junior year, Brock left the university to play in the Major Leagues. He began his career with the Chicago Cubs in 1961. Brock retired from the Cardinals in 1979. He has been honored with a star on the St. Louis Walk of Fame; a statue outside of Busch Stadium; induction into the state halls of fame in Arkansas, Louisiana, and Missouri; and numerous other awards.

PHOTO COURTESY OF JOHN A. WRIGHT SR.

PHOTO COURTESY OF MERCANTILE LIBRARY AT UMSL

Grace Bumbry

1937–

INTERNATIONAL OPERA SINGER

race Bumbry, one of the most universally acclaimed opera stars of our time, was born in St. Louis in 1937. While still a student at Sumner High School and under the tutelage of Kenneth Billups in the Sumner a capella choir, Bumbry won her first big talent competition, earning a scholarship to the now-defunct St. Louis Institute of Music, which refused to let her attend classes because of her race. The school did offer her private lessons, but her parents refused. Soon afterward, Bumbry appeared on Arthur Godfrey's nationally televised talent scout program, where Godfrey predicted that Bumbry would become "one of the most famous names in music." Later, she won a scholarship to Northwestern University, where she became a protégé of the celebrated Lotte Lehmann, a famous, German-born opera star. Bumbry also studied at Boston University and the Music Academy of the West in Santa Barbara, California.

Bumbry began her rise to operatic stardom in 1960, when she made her debut at the Paris Opera as Amneris in *Aida* and became an instant star. In 1961, Bumbry became the first African American singer to perform at the Bayreuth Festival, a German event that celebrated the works of Richard Wagner. Some individuals there first objected because of her race, but in the end, Bumbry's performance as Venus in *Tannhauser* was a huge success.

In 1963, Bumbry made her United States debut at the Chicago Lyric Opera, again as Wagner's Venus. She also has played leading roles in Gershwin's *Porgy and Bess*, Verdi's *Macbeth*, and Strauss's *Salome*. Bumbry went on to sing dramatic mezzo and, later, soprano roles, in all of the world's great opera houses, becoming one of the most sought-after performers of her time. Her voice repeatedly has been praised for its wide range and rich color.

Bumbry retired from the stage in 1979. She now sings in concerts and teaches students around the world. In 2009, she was honored at the Kennedy Center for the Performing Arts in Washington, D.C., for her lifetime of work.

$\mathcal{I}$vory Crockett

1948–

WORLD'S FASTEST HUMAN

$\mathcal{O}$n May 11, 1974, Ivory Crockett arrived in Knoxville, Tennessee, to run in a 100-yard dash. He had been sprinting competitively for nearly ten years and he was tired. Plus, Crockett was having a difficult time psyching himself up for yet another race. Just before the race, reportedly Crockett wrote down a time of 8.9 seconds and tucked the paper in the bottom of his track shoe. The gun sounded, and Crockett set off, competing against some of the nation's fastest runners.

On that day, Crockett set a new world record of 9.0 seconds, making him the world's fastest human. The record will stand forever, because 100-yard dash races are no longer held.

Crockett was born in 1948 in Webster Groves, Missouri. He graduated from Webster Groves High School in 1968, where he set almost every track record. He was equally good at football, but track was his first love. Crockett's goal in high school was to run the 100-yard dash in 9.5 seconds. He achieved that and was the second-fastest high school sprinter in the country.

After graduation, Crockett enrolled at Southern Illinois University in Carbondale, where he continued sprinting at meets around the country. In 1969, he won the Amateur Athletic Union's Championship in Miami, Florida. Then, at the Olympic trials semifinals in 1974, Crockett suffered two pulled hamstrings. The previous year, Crockett had considered playing professional football with the New Orleans Saints but was reluctant to lose his

IVORY
CROCKETT
PARK

amateur athlete status, which would make him ineligible for the Olympics. But now, he had to drop out of competition and hang up his spikes.

In 1968, the city of Webster Groves recognized Crockett by naming a park at Bell and Almentor avenues in North Webster in his honor. In 2004, the Webster Groves School District founded the "Ivory Crockett Run 4 Webster" to honor him, inspired by Crockett's desire to give something back to the community. Proceeds from the annual event benefit students in the Webster Groves School District.

*G*erald Early

1952–
PROFESSOR AND AUTHOR

*G*erald Early is a nationally recognized writer and one of St. Louis's most accomplished intellectual figures. He serves as the Merle Kling Professor of Modern Letters, professor of English, and chair of the Department of African and African-American Studies at Washington University. He was the founding director of the Center for the Humanities at the university, which promotes St. Louis as a center of intellectual inquiry by sponsoring innovative public conferences on such topics as Midwestern Black history, authors and scientists, and Black-Jewish relations. Early also is the author and editor of more than a dozen books on such diverse topics as jazz, comics, African-American literature, baseball, and boxing.

A native of Philadelphia, Early was born to a baker and preschool teacher. He developed a love for literature at an early age. He received his bachelor's degree from the University of Pennsylvania and his master's and doctorate degrees in English literature from Cornell University.

Since the beginning of his career, Early has been recognized and honored for his work in the literary arts. In 1988, Early received the Whiting Prize and earned a General Electric Foundation Award for Younger Writers. His work was included in *The Best American Essays 1986* as well as several subsequent volumes in that series. In

PORTRAIT BY JAMIE ADAMS

PHOTO COURTESY OF GERALD EARLY

1995, he won a National Book Critics Circle Award for Criticism for *The Culture of Bruising,* his book of essays on prizefighting, and his book *Daughters: On Family and Fatherhood* was a semifinalist.

Early twice has been nominated for the Grammy Award in the category of Best Album Notes, for *Yes I Can: The Sammy Davis, Jr. Story* (2000) and for *Rhapsodies in Black; Music and Words from the Harlem Renaissance* (2001). For the academic year 2001–02, Early was an invited fellow at the National Humanities Center in North Carolina, where he worked on a book about African Americans and the Korean War.

A frequent guest on National Public Radio and an expert on Black athletes, Early appeared in Ken Burns's PBS documentary series *Baseball* and in two HBO documentaries, *The Journey of the African American Athlete* and a special about Sonny Liston. In recognition of his many accomplishments, Washington University has placed the above portrait of Early in the campus library among other well-known writers. He is the first African American so honored. He also is honored on the St. Louis Walk of Fame.

Cedric the Entertainer

1964–

ACTOR, COMEDIAN, AND DIRECTOR

Cedric Antonio Kyles is widely known by his stage name, Cedric the Entertainer. Roles in films such as *Barbershop*, *Be Cool, Madagascar, Intolerable Cruelty*, and *The Johnson Family Vacation* (which he starred in and produced) have allowed Cedric to live up to his moniker and truly entertain on a global level.

Born in 1964 in Jefferson City, Missouri, Cedric was brought up in Caruthersville, Missouri. After junior high school, his family moved to Berkeley, a suburb of St. Louis, where Cedric graduated from Berkeley High School. Cedric continued his education at Southeast Missouri State University, where he majored in mass communication. Before becoming a full-time comedian, Cedric worked as a high school teacher and as a claims adjuster for State Farm Insurance.

In 2001, more than 144 million viewers saw Cedric in the Bud Light commercial that landed in the No. 1 spot during the Super Bowl broadcast. In January 2002, he published a book, *Grown-Ass Man*. In 2006, Cedric's HBO Comedy Special *Cedric the Entertainer, Taking You Higher*, was the highest-rated special of that year for the network.

Cedric's work in the entertainment world has garnered him numerous accolades and awards. In addition to being on the St.

PHOTO COURTESY OF ERIC RHONE

CEDRIC AT ST. LOUIS SISTER CITY AIDS FUNDRAISER,
PHOTO COURTESY OF JOHN A. WRIGHT SR.

Louis Walk of Fame, Cedric has won four consecutive NAACP Image Awards and the AFTRA Award of Excellence in Television.

In 1995, Cedric established the Cedric the Entertainer Charitable Foundation, Inc., as a way to give back to his community. The foundation—with the motto "Reaching Out . . . Giving Back"—has awarded more than one hundred scholarships and countless incentives to Berkeley High School students and graduates, and Cedric plans to extend the foundation's reach to a national audience. Cedric now is head of his own production company, A Bird and a Bear Entertainment, where he develops and produces feature films. He made his directorial debut with the dance-film spoof *Dance Fu*. In 2011, he launched his own WhoCed line of designer hats, and in 2012, he introduced his new TV Land sitcom, *The Soul Man*. Since 2018 he has been the star of *The Neighbourhood*.

$\mathcal{R}$edd Foxx

1922–1991
COMEDIAN

*J*ohn Elroy Sanford, better known as Redd Foxx, was a groundbreaking comic. He joked about everything from sex to race, in language that was considered offensive by many. His style of bringing taboo issues into the open helped paved the way for comedians that followed him, and he opened the door for many Black comedians.

Sanford was born into poverty in St. Louis on December 9, 1922. Because of his ruddy complexion, he gained the nickname Redd. His last name, Foxx, was derived from a much-admired baseball player named Jimmie Foxx. When he was thirteen, Redd Foxx left St. Louis for Chicago, where he supported himself by singing and playing a washboard string bass with bands that performed on street corners. After three years, when his band broke up, Foxx hopped a train and headed for New York with some of the band members. There, again they performed on street corners until they were discovered and asked to perform on *Major Bowes Amateur Hour*, a radio talent show.

The band went on to perform at the Apollo Theater and nightspots in Brooklyn and New Jersey. Things were going well until Foxx had some problems with the law and had to spend time in jail. At that point, half the band headed home.

Once out of jail, Foxx began his solo career in comedy. In the early years, he performed mostly in Black clubs and theaters. By the 1950s, his career was well underway, and he performed

Photo courtesy of John A. Wright Sr.

Photo courtesy of Mercantile Library at UMSL

stand-up comedy on the nightclub circuit. He soon recorded his first live long-playing record, *Laff of the Party*, which became one of the biggest party hit albums of all time. His good fortune continued, and throughout his career Foxx released more than fifty comedy albums.

In 1972, Foxx got a major break. He signed a contract with Norman Lear to appear in a new television sitcom called *Sanford and Son*. The show was a huge success and ran for five seasons. In 1977, Foxx hosted his own variety show on ABC, *The Redd Foxx Comedy Hour*, which lasted just one season. He later made two other unsuccessful sitcoms and then left television for a while during the 1980s. In 1991, Foxx tried to make a comeback as part of the cast for the television show *The Royal Family*. During rehearsal, Foxx suffered a heart attack and died at the age of sixty-eight.

Chester Arthur Franklin

1880–1955

PUBLISHER

With a dream and much determination, in 1919 Chester Arthur Franklin founded the *Call*, the leading African American newspaper in Kansas City to this day. Franklin began his journalism career under the tutelage of his father, George Franklin, who owned the *Colorado Statesman* newspaper. Later, the paper was renamed the *Star*.

Chester Franklin, or C.A. as his close friends called him, was born on June 7, 1880, in Denison, Texas, to Clara Belle Williams Franklin, a teacher, and his father, who was a barber at the time. After young Franklin graduated from high school in Omaha, he attended the University of Nebraska for two years, when the elder Franklin became too ill to operate the paper. Chester moved to Denver and took over the business. He continued to publish the paper with his mother until 1913, when he moved to Kansas City. Residents of Denver hated to see him leave because Franklin was active in politics and in the community, and he also was responsible for the hiring of the first African American in a white-collar job in government service in Denver.

Kansas City had a larger African American community than Denver, but World War I delayed Franklin's career plans. First, Franklin opened a printing shop, and on May 6, 1919, he founded the *Call*, which long has served as a voice of the Black community. The first year in business, Franklin encountered a

Inside
THE CALL
National
Women's
History Month
Theme
See page 8

Snowfalls Rank Second Among
All Time February Totals

number of obstacles. When the printers' union would not allow any experienced printers to work for Franklin, he and his assistant learned to operate the press on their own.

The first issue of the paper was four pages, and two thousand copies sold in the first week. Franklin first sold subscriptions to friends at the YMCA, and then his mother went door to door in the evening, selling subscriptions to boost circulation. The paper's popularity grew. In 1925, Franklin married Ada Crogman, who also went to work for the newspaper.

As publisher and editor of the *Call*, Franklin always took an interest in the civic life of the community, and he was active in the establishment of Wheatley-Provident Hospital and the building of the Paseo YMCA. Franklin died in 1955. His legacy was continued at the *Call* by his wife and by editor Lucy Bluford, the first African American to graduate from the University of Kansas School of Journalism.

Robert Guillaume

1927–2017

ACTOR, SINGER, AND MOVIE PRODUCER

obert Guillaume, known for his television and stage acting careers, was born Robert Peter Williams on November 30, 1927, in St. Louis. As an adult, he chose the name "Guillaume," the French translation for "Williams," because he felt it would be distinctive.

Guillaume's father left the family when the boy was very young, and he went to live with his grandmother, whom he credited for teaching him the meaning of family. He attended St. Nicholas Elementary School and St. Joseph High School, where he was expelled from ninth grade. Guillaume later enlisted in the US Army. After a brief stint, he resigned with an honorable discharge and returned to St. Louis, where he finished high school.

After graduation, Guillaume tried his hand at a number of jobs while attending evening classes at Saint Louis University. Although his original goal was a degree in business administration, by his mid-twenties, Guillaume aspired to be a performer. He received a scholarship from Washington University in St. Louis to study in Aspen, Colorado, and while there, he was invited to perform at the Karamu Theater in Cleveland. At Karamu he performed in *Carousel*. That led him to Broadway, where he appeared in the musical *Free and Easy*, his first paying job. After the show closed, Guillaume toured Europe with Quincy Jones and later made two cross-country tours in the show *Purlie*.

Guillaume began his television career with guest appearances, and later played permanent characters in *Soap* and in its spin-off *Benson*, where he played the title character. He received the Best Supporting Actor Emmy Award for *Soap* and a Best Lead Actor Emmy Award for *Benson*, which gave him the distinction of being the only actor in the history of television to receive two awards for playing the same character.

Guillaume's greatest theatrical achievement occurred in 1990, when he became the only African American to perform the lead role in Andrew Lloyd Webber's Broadway musical *Phantom of the Opera*. Many critics were upset to see an African American playing a role previously performed by a white actor, but due to Guillaume's fine performance, the complaints quickly stopped.

In 1994, he lent his voice to the character of Rafiki in Disney's animated movie *The Lion King*. Five years later, Guillaume suffered a stroke in his dressing room while working as one of the stars in Aaron Sorkin's HBO series *Sports Night*. Because of quick medical attention, the effects of the stroke were minimized, and Guillaume returned to the show.

Prior to his death in 2017, Guillaume was a philanthropist and also served as a spokesman for the American Heart Association and the American Stroke Association. Besides his two Emmy Awards, Guillaume also is the winner of four NAACP Image Awards and he is on the St. Louis Walk of Fame.

W.C. Handy

1871–1958

MUSICIAN, COMPOSER, MUSICAL HISTORIAN, AND CHORAL AND ORCHESTRAL CONDUCTOR

*I*n 1893, William Christopher Handy traveled by boxcar from Chicago to St. Louis, where he spent many lonely, hungry nights on the cobblestone levee. Those nights taught him about the sights and sounds of the riverfront, and years later, his experiences inspired "St. Louis Blues," his most celebrated song.

Handy composed and first performed the world-famous song in 1914 at Pee Wee's Saloon on Beale Street in Memphis, where Handy's band was headquartered at the time. Handy, who in his lifetime composed more than 150 songs, became known as the "Father of the Blues." In 1931, the city of Memphis honored Handy by creating the W.C. Handy Park on Beale Street.

Handy was born in a log cabin on November 16, 1871, in Florence, Alabama. As a youngster, he created music with broom handles, harmonicas, combs, and earthenware jugs. He once saved enough money to buy a guitar, but his father ordered him to trade it for a dictionary. In his autobiography, *Father of the Blues*, Handy recalled his father saying, "Son I'd rather see you in a hearse, I'd rather follow you to the graveyard, than to hear you had become a musician."

Because Handy wanted a career in music, he left home at fifteen to join Mahara's Minstrels, a traveling revue. Handy returned home when the show ran out of money, but he left again in 1886,

carrying just twenty cents in his pocket. He traveled throughout the Midwest, taking odd jobs and teaching and performing music.

Handy's first big hit was "Memphis Blues," written in 1912. It was the first copyrighted blues song, and Handy sold the rights for a mere fifty dollars. Handy wised up the second time around. Refusing the small fees offered for the rights to "St. Louis Blues," Handy, with the help of a friend, published the song himself. Jazz vocalist Ethel Waters popularized the song on the vaudeville circuit, and in 1917, Sophie Tucker—known as "The Last of the Red Hot Mamas"—recorded the song. The Russian-born Tucker was one of the top singers in America in the early twentieth century, and sales of "St. Louis Blues" exceed one million copies, a first for a blues song.

Handy later explained that when he wrote "St. Louis Blues," he took "the humor of the coon song, the syncopation of ragtime and the spirit of the Negro folk song and called it a blues." The composition changed his life forever. As Handy put it, "I was forty the year when 'St. Louis Blues' was published, and ever since then my life has revolved around the composition."

Handy developed a serious eye condition and was blind by 1943, but he continued to compose and publish music through the Handy Brothers Music Company, where he served as president and treasurer. Handy died on March 28, 1958, of acute bronchial pneumonia.

Ron Himes

1952–

ACTOR, REPERTORY COMPANY FOUNDER, AND PRODUCER

*R*on Himes is the founder and producing director of the St. Louis Black Repertory Company and the Henry E. Hampton Jr. Artist-in-Residence at Washington University in St. Louis. Born on June 3, 1952, in St. Louis, Himes is the son of Johnny James Himes, a foundry worker, and Vivian Mae Himes, a laundress.

When he was six years old, Himes announced he wanted to be an aeronautical engineer and held on to that desire for several years. As an eighth grader Himes attended programs at the YMCA on the Washington University campus. Himes grew attached to the campus, and he enrolled after high school. He was pre-med, then pre-law, and he also studied Eastern philosophy, psychology, and sociology. Himes graduated in 1978 with a degree of business administration from Washington University's College in Arts and Sciences.

While still a student, Himes founded the Black Repertory Company in 1976. The company began touring to other campuses and in 1981 found a home at the Greeley Presbyterian Church in North St. Louis, which eventually was converted and renamed the 23rd Street Theatre. In 1991, the company moved to the Grand Center Arts and Education District in St. Louis's Midtown neighborhood, taking over the multimillion-dollar former First Congregational Church.

The company has grown into one of the most influential theater companies in the country, producing plays and musicals

from an African American perspective. Himes has produced and directed over two hundred plays, including all ten written by August Wilson; and also the world premiere of *The Montford Point Marine* by Samm-Art Williams, produced at the Black Rep in 2011.

Himes was selected as the very first Henry E. Hampton Jr. Artist-in-Residence at Washington University in 2003, in conjunction with the Performing Arts and African American Studies departments. In 2010, he helped lead the US delegation to the Third World Festival of Black Arts and Culture in Dakar, Senegal. Himes has been the recipient of multiple awards and honors, including a 2007 Distinguished Alumni Award from the University College at Washington University; a St. Louis 2004 Heroes Pierre Laclede Award; and Honorary Doctorate of Fine Arts degrees from the University of Missouri–St. Louis in 1993 and from Washington University in 1997.

$\mathcal{L}$angston Hughes

1902–1967

POET, SOCIAL ACTIVIST, NOVELIST, PLAYWRIGHT, AND
COLUMNIST

ames Langston Hughes was the most prolific African American writer of his era from the time of his first pioneer poems, *The Weary Blues*, published in 1926, through 1967, the year of his death. For his prodigious literary output, Hughes became known as "Shakespeare in Harlem" and "The Poet Laureate of the Negro Race."

Hughes wrote sixteen books of poetry, two novels, three short story collections, twenty plays, four volumes of "editorial" and "documentary" fiction, musicals and operas, poetry for children, three autobiographies, a dozen radio and television scripts, and dozens of magazine articles.

Hughes was born in 1902 in Joplin, Missouri. His father left home shortly after his birth, and he went to live with his grandmother, Mary Langston, in Lawrence, Kansas, where he spent most of his childhood. His grandfather, Charles Henry Langston, was an abolitionist who was killed while fighting at Harper's Ferry. After his grandmother passed, Hughes went to live with his mother and stepfather in Lincoln, Illinois, where he wrote his first verse and was selected class poet.

The family soon moved to Cleveland, Ohio, where Hughes attended high school. At the end of his junior year, he was invited by his father to join him in Mexico. On his way there, traveling by train, Hughes wrote his famous poem, "The Negro

Speaks of Rivers," which was published in *The Crisis*, a publication of the NAACP. Hughes stayed in Mexico for one summer, and then returned to Cleveland to finish high school. After graduation, he enrolled at Columbia University but dropped out after a year to pursue his writing.

In 1923, Hughes traveled aboard a freighter to West Africa, Europe, and Russia. One of his favorite pastimes, whether he was abroad or in the US, was sitting in clubs listening to blues and jazz while writing poetry. Based on a conversation with an acquaintance in a Harlem bar, Hughes created a character known as My Simple Minded Friend, later renamed Jess B. Simple. The character was featured in a series of Hughes's essays written in the form of a dialogue.

Hughes's genius was discovered and developed during the Harlem Renaissance in New York, where Hughes brought the Black experience to American literature. He also used Black folk material to protest the treatment and conditions of African Americans in United States. Hughes died on May 22, 1967. His home at 20 East 127th Street in Harlem has been designated a landmark by the New York City Preservation Commission.

$\mathcal{J}$ulius Hunter

1943–

NEWS ANCHOR, JOURNALIST, AUTHOR, AND MUSICIAN

$\mathcal{J}$ulius Hunter was described as the "consummate pro" journalist by the late titan of American journalism, Walter Cronkite. Hunter is among very few American journalists who have conducted exclusive, one-on-one interviews with five incumbent US presidents—Gerald Ford, Jimmy Carter, Ronald Reagan, George Bush Sr., and Bill Clinton—and traveled three times with Pope John Paul II. Hunter is much more, quoting a published news article, "He is also a writer, a radio talk-show host, a columnist and a musician." Hunter has conducted the St. Louis Symphony Orchestra several times. He is the founder of Julius K. Hunter and Friends African American Research Collection at the St. Louis County Library in St. Louis, a major resource for those doing genealogical research.

Hunter celebrated thirty-three years in broadcasting that included senior anchor and reporter at KMOV-TV-Channel 4 and reporter at KSDK-News Channel 5. At KMOX-TV he was the first African American assigned to a primetime position in St. Louis. Throughout his career he was deeply involved in the education of children. While at KMOV-TV he was the host and initiator of the *Do the Right Thing* program, which recognized metro-area children who made outstanding contributions to their homes, schools, and communities and exemplified the teachings of Dr. Martin Luther King Jr. He also hosted the *Young Heroes in Music* radio program, which featured promising young African

American musicians, and *Julius Hunter's Reflections*, a weekly cable-television program.

Hunter has been a dedicated mentor to young students seeking careers in broadcast journalism and is a published author whose works include everything from a children's alphabet book to a broadcast journalism college textbook. After retiring from broadcasting, Hunter worked as vice president for communications at Saint Louis University for five years.

Hunter has been the recipient of numerous awards for his services and work, including an appointment by Governor Matt Blunt to the St. Louis Board of Police Commissioners.

Hunter is a product of the St. Louis Public Schools, a graduate of Sumner High School and Harris Teachers College (now Harris-Stowe State University), where he composed his alma mater's anthem. After earning his B.A. degree from Harris, he was a teacher in the district for three years.

$\mathcal{S}$cott Joplin

1868–1917
RAGTIME COMPOSER AND PIANIST

$\mathcal{S}$cott Joplin, perhaps the pre-eminent ragtime composer in the world, was born into a musical family on November 24, 1868, in Texarkana, Texas. Young Joplin first played the family guitar and for a time blew a bugle in a local band. His natural talent was most dramatically revealed when he sat down to play a piano in a neighbor's home. In spite of the family's poverty, Joplin's father bought an old piano, and by the time the boy was eleven, he had become a proficient player and improviser.

In 1885, when Joplin was seventeen, he traveled to St. Louis. There, he played and gathered with other pianists at the Silver Dollar Saloon, owned by John Turpin, the father of Tom Turpin, who is credited as the first African American to publish a lively form of music known as a rag. Tom Turpin was no doubt a strong source of inspiration as well as a good friend to Joplin.

After absorbing the St. Louis nightlife, Joplin traveled to Sedalia, Missouri, where he was employed as a pianist at the Maple Leaf Club. While there, Joplin reorganized the Texas Medley Quartette, which traveled as far as Syracuse, New York. He sold his first two compositions—"A Picture of Her Face" and "Please Say You Will"—to New York publishers.

In 1897, the band's second but final tour ended in the town of Joplin, where the band was dissolved. Joplin remained in town and wrote "Maple Leaf," his most important rag. Through

promotions by publisher John Stark, in six months more than 75,000 copies of the sheet music had been sold.

Now successful, Joplin married and moved back to St. Louis. He gave up his nightclub gigs, became a much-respected teacher, and produced nineteen piano pieces. Joplin's greatest desire was to produce an opera. He tried twice, with *A Guest of Honor* and *Treemonisha*. Neither was well received. After several unsuccessful attempts with *Treemonisha*, Joplin became heartbroken and fell into a depression. In 1916, his wife realized that his condition was hopeless and had him committed to the Manhattan State Hospital in New York, where he died on April 1, 1917.

Treemonisha was rediscovered in 1970, and it was produced in 1972 as a joint production of the music department of Morehouse College and the Atlanta Symphony Orchestra in Atlanta, Georgia. Since then, Joplin's opera has been performed all over the United States, including at the St. Louis Opera, the Houston Grand Opera, the Kennedy Center in Washington, D.C., and on Broadway, always to overwhelming critical and public acclaim. In 1976, Joplin was posthumously awarded a Pulitzer Prize for "contributions to American music."

The Scott Joplin House State Historic Site, under the auspices of the Missouri State Parks, stands at 2658 Delmar Boulevard in St. Louis.

Albert King

1923–1992

SONGWRITER, MUSICIAN, AND PRODUCER

When the definitive history of the guitar is written, Albert King will be among the major musicians discussed because of his profound impact on the sound of blues, rock and roll, and soul.

One of thirteen children, King was born Albert Nelson on a cotton plantation on April 25, 1923, in Indianola, Mississippi. He was introduced to music by singing in a church gospel group where his father played the guitar. As a child King would listen to family records and spend hours trying to duplicate the sound of well-known artists of the day on his homemade cigar box guitars and diddley-bows. He received his first real guitar in 1942. He taught himself how to play the instrument upside-down while keeping the strings strung for a right-handed player. He would play with his thumb, as opposed to a pick, and he became a master of the single-string solo. Over time, King developed a style that set him apart from his contemporaries.

King's career began near Osceola, Arkansas, where he performed with a group known as the Groove Boys. He later moved to St. Louis, and the late 1940s found him in Gary, Indiana, where he played alongside established guitarists Jimmy Reed and John Brim. In 1953, in Chicago, King made his first recordings—"Bad Luck Blues" and "Be On Your Merry Way"—on the Parrot label. The recordings found modest regional success but reaped little financial benefit for King, so he returned to St.

Louis where there was a thriving blues scene. King took up the "Gibson Flying V" model electric guitar, which he named "Lucy," and that became his trademark instrument.

King then moved to Memphis in 1966, and his career took off after he signed with Stax Records and recorded the classic "Born Under a Bad Sign." King's music crossed over to other genres and he recorded with rock musicians, on tribute albums, and even with comedians. In 1969, King became the first blues musician to perform in concert with a symphony orchestra when he appeared at Powell Hall with the St. Louis Symphony Orchestra.

A prolific musician, King recorded and performed regularly until the mid-1980s. He was a major influence on the next generation of guitarists, including Jimi Hendrix, Eric Clapton, Stevie Ray Vaughan, and Robert Cray.

King suffered a heart attack and died on December 21, 1992, just two days after performing in Los Angeles. King is a member of the Blues Foundation Hall of Fame, and his songs "Born Under a Bad Sign" and "Live Wire Blues Power" have been honored as Classics of Blues Recordings.

$\mathcal{S}$onny Liston

1932–1971
BOXER

$\mathcal{S}$onny Liston, Heavyweight Champion of the World (1962–1964), was the son of Tobey Liston, a tenant farmer, and his second wife, Helen. The twenty-fourth of his father's twenty-five children, the boy was born on May 8, 1932, in St. Francis County, Arkansas. As a youngster, Liston worked in the local cotton fields. When he was thirteen, he moved to St. Louis to live with an aunt. Once in St. Louis, Liston immediately got into difficulty with the law and was arrested numerous times. In 1950, he was convicted of two counts of larceny and two counts of first-degree robbery and was sent to the Missouri State Penitentiary for more than two years.

While in prison, Liston was introduced to the sport of boxing. Once paroled in 1952, Liston embarked on his world-renowned boxing career, winning local, regional, national, and international Golden Glove titles.

In 1953, Liston turned professional and went on to have a series of successful bouts. Then his career was interrupted for nine months in December 1956, when he was sent to the St. Louis Workhouse for assaulting a policeman and stealing the officer's gun. After his release, Liston moved to Philadelphia, where after twenty-five consecutive boxing bouts he earned an opportunity to fight Heavyweight Champion Floyd Patterson on September 25, 1962.

After two minutes, Liston knocked out Patterson—and for the first time in history, a reigning heavyweight champion was counted out in the first round. In a rematch the following summer, Liston had another successful bout, winning with a knockout.

After a seventeen-month reign as heavyweight champion, Liston lost his title when he was knocked down by a right-handed punch from Cassius Clay in a first round that lasted one minute and forty-five seconds. After his loss to Clay (now Muhammad Ali), Liston began a comeback, winning eleven consecutive fights by knockouts before losing to Leotis Martin. Liston returned to the ring and registered a win with a tenth-round technical knockout against Chuck Wepner.

On January 5, 1971, Liston was found dead of an apparent drug overdose in his home in Nevada. His career record was 50–4 with thirty-nine knockouts. In 1991, he was inducted into the International boxing Hall of Fame.

Robert McFerrin Sr.

1921–2006
OPERA SINGER

Helen Phillips

1920–2005
OPERA SINGER

Robert Keith McFerrin Sr. and Helen Phillips were pioneers in the opera world. They broke color barriers and opened doors for the many African Americans who followed in their footsteps.

McFerrin was born in 1921, in Marianna, Arkansas, the seventh of eight children. He began his musical education singing in the choir at his father's church. He came to St. Louis, attended public schools, and graduated from Sumner High School. He went on to earn a bachelor of music degree from Chicago Musical College.

McFerrin sang on Broadway and with the National Negro Opera Company, and in 1953 he became the Metropolitan Opera's first African American male soloist. McFerrin provided the vocals for Sidney Poitier in the 1959 film classic *Porgy and Bess*. He toured and taught internationally before returning to St. Louis in 1973.

A severe stroke in 1989 impaired McFerrin's verbal ability, but not his singing voice. He courageously resumed performances, including concerts with his highly acclaimed son, Bobby McFerrin. He kept a demanding schedule until 1998, when his

increasing disabilities forced his retirement. He died in 2006 after a long illness.

Helen Phillips was born in 1920 in St. Louis, where she attended public schools. While at Sumner High School, she was discovered and her talent was developed by Mr. Wirt Walton, her music teacher. After graduation, Phillips entered Lincoln University on a scholarship from Delta Sigma Theta Sorority. Because of her singing ability, she was asked to assist with beginners in the music department. Subsequently, Phillips studied two years at Fisk University and two years at the Kroeger School of Music in St. Louis.

In 1947, Phillips became the first African American singer to appear with the Metropolitan Opera Chorus. Phillips also was the first African American soloist to perform with Edwin Franko Goldman's band, which played in Central Park in the 1940s and 1950s. After World War II, Phillips made more than five hundred concert appearances in Austria and West Germany for the US State Department. She made her Town Hall debut in 1953 in New York City.

Later in her career, Phillips became a schoolteacher and a vocal coach. She died in 2005 of heart failure.

Patricia McKissack

1944–2017

Fredrick McKissack

1939–2013
AUTHORS

Patricia C. and Fredrick McKissack, two of Missouri's most prolific children's book authors, wrote and published more than one hundred books on the African American experience. As individuals and as a team, the McKissacks' books have earned the Coretta Scott King Award (1990, 1993, and 1995), the Horn Nook Award in 1992, the Newbery Honor Award in 1993, the Orbis Pictus Award in 1995, and the Pen/Steven Kroll Award in 2012. The McKissacks' books for young people focus on the history and experiences of African Americans, using fiction, history, and biography to tell stories in an informative and entertaining manner on a wide array of topics.

Patricia was born on August 9, 1944, in Smyrna, Tennessee, to Robert and Emma Carwell. She gave her mother credit for inspiring her to write and recalled that her father and grandparents often would tell her stories about smart and brave individuals. Many of those stories have become part of her books. After high school, Patricia attended the University of Georgia, where she encountered Fredrick McKissack, a childhood friend. They married in 1965. For a time, Patricia taught English to junior high

students, but in 1971, she decided she wanted to be an author. Her first book was a biography of Paul Lawrence Dunbar.

Fredrick was born in Nashville, the son of architect Lewis W. and Bessie Fizer McKissack. After a stint in the US Marine Corps from 1957 to 1960, Frederick enrolled in Tennessee Agricultural and Industrial State University. He graduated with a bachelor of science degree in 1965, the same year he married Patricia. The couple moved to St. Louis, where Fredrick worked as a civil engineer for the city and the federal government until 1974, when he established his own contracting firm.

Soon after, Fredrick began collaborating with Patricia on books. In 1982, he became a full-time writer and operator of All-Writing Services in partnership with her. The two worked as a team, with Fredrick doing most of the research and fact-checking and Patricia the writing.

$\mathcal{A}$rchie Moore

1916–1998
LIGHT HEAVYWEIGHT WORLD CHAMPION

$\mathcal{K}$nown as "The Old Mongoose" and a master of the ring with one of the biggest professional careers in the history of sports, Archie Moore logged over two hundred professional fights and holds the record for the most career knockouts (141). Born Archibald Lee Wright in Benoit, Mississippi, he was brought up in St. Louis by his aunt and uncle, Pearl and Cleveland Moore, and took their surname.

After the untimely deaths of his uncle and sister, Moore entered a rebellious period. As Moore recalls in his 1960 autobiography, *The Archie Moore Story*, after he began stealing from his family and in his neighborhood, he was sentenced to the Missouri Training School in Boonville for two years. Burdened by feelings of shame, Moore was changed by that experience. While there, he learned that professional fighters could make $750 in one night, so Moore took up boxing. He began training in the school gym and scored sixteen knockout wins in his first year of intramural matches.

After seventeen years as a professional boxer, Moore got a shot at the light heavyweight championship against Joey Maxim in 1952. He defeated Maxim in the fifteenth round. A decade later, a ring-weary Moore took on a match for the money with Cassius Clay (later known as Muhammad Ali), who knocked him

out in the fourth round. Moore ended his fighting career and worked as an actor in television and film. He also trained fighters and assisted George Foreman for his fight against Ali in Zaire in 1974.

In 1998, Moore died in his adopted home of San Diego, California, holding the rank of fourth on *Ring Magazine*'s list of 100 Greatest Punchers. The prominent boxing website BoxRec called Moore "the greatest pound-for-pound boxer of all time."

$\mathcal{B}$uck O'Neil

1911–2006
BASEBALL PLAYER

$\mathcal{J}$ohn Jordan "Buck" O'Neil, a Negro League pioneer and posthumous Presidential Medal of Freedom recipient, was born November 13, 1911, in Carrabelle, Florida. O'Neil's father, who played for local teams, introduced the boy to baseball at an early age. He was nicknamed "Buck" after Buck O'Neal, co-owner of the Miami Giants. The family moved to Sarasota and, by the time he was twelve, young O'Neil was playing semi-pro baseball.

Because of segregation in Sarasota, he was not allowed to attend the local high school, so O'Neil enrolled in Edward Waters College in Jacksonville, where he earned his high school diploma and attended two years of college. He then left school to play pro baseball with a barnstorming team called the Zulu Cannibal Giants, where O'Neil wore war paint and a grass skirt.

Segregation also kept O'Neil out of Major League baseball, so he took his talent to the Negro Leagues and joined the Kansas City Monarchs in 1938. A decade later, he was named player-manager for the Monarchs and continued his affiliation with the club until the end of the 1955 season.

O'Neil had a career batting average of .288, including four .300-plus seasons at the plate. He led the league in batting twice, hitting .345 in 1940 and .350 in 1946, and he played in three Negro American League All-Star games and two Negro American League World Series. At the height of the Negro League

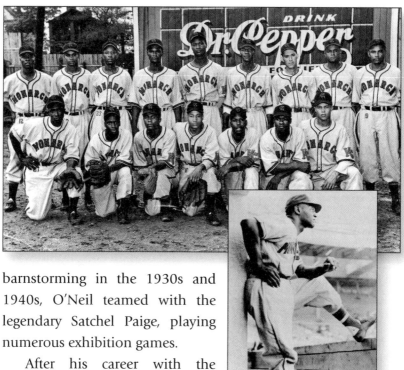

barnstorming in the 1930s and 1940s, O'Neil teamed with the legendary Satchel Paige, playing numerous exhibition games.

After his career with the Monarchs, O'Neil joined Major League Baseball in 1955 as a part-time scout for the Chicago Cubs. By 1962, he was a full-time coach, the first African American to be officially designated as such. O'Neil received many honors for his accomplishments. In 1995, the Baltimore Orioles renamed a training facility in Sarasota The Buck O'Neil Baseball Complex, and Sarasota High School presented O'Neil with a diploma to make amends for the one he was denied many years ago.

O'Neil was one of the true pioneers of the Negro Baseball Leagues and also a co-founder and chairman of the Negro Leagues Baseball Museum in Kansas City, Missouri. After his death in 2006, he was presented with the Presidential Medal of Freedom. Two years later, O'Neil was inducted into the National Baseball Hall of Fame.

$\mathcal{N}$elly

1974–

*G*rammy Award winner Cornell Ira Haynes Jr., better known as Nelly, was born November 3, 1974, in Austin, Texas. With his family, he moved to St. Louis and later to University City, a suburban community west of the city, where he attended University City High School. While there, he demonstrated outstanding skill in baseball and considered making it a career, but after his efforts to get into the Major Leagues failed, he turned to music.

In the mid-1990s, Nelly and his friends, who had been writing and rapping together, formed a group known as the St. Lunatics. They produced a regional hit, "Gimmie What You Got," which received a great deal of notice but failed to develop into a major record deal. Nelly later signed a contract with Universal Records and produced his solo album *Country Grammar*, which became a Top 10 hit. The album rose to No. 1 on the Billboard 200, selling over 360,000 copies in its first week.

That was just the beginning. *Country Grammar* became one of the biggest-selling albums in music history when it hit the nine million mark, topping the charts for several weeks. This album put Nelly well on his way to becoming an American icon and one of the top recording artists of his generation.

Nelly has since produced a number of top-selling albums and singles. The Recording Industry Association of American has ranked Nelly as one of the best-selling male artists in American

PHOTO COURTESY OF DERRTY ENTERTAINMENT,
PHOTOGRAPH BY MARC BAPTISTE

music history, with over twenty-one million albums sold in the United States. Nelly has been recognized by St. Louis with a star on the Walk of Fame.

Nelly made his movie debut with a supporting role in the 2005 remake *The Longest Yard*, starring Adam Sandler and Chris Rock. Cashing in on his success in the movie, Nelly started his own clothing lines: Vokal for men and Apple Bottoms for women. He also created an energy drink. Nelly has appeared on television shows, a Super Bowl halftime show, and a host of magazine covers. Nelly also has ventured into other enterprises through part-ownership of the Charlotte Bobcats of the National Baseball Association, controlling interest in a National Association for Stock Car Auto Racing Team, and his own recording label, Derrty Enterprise.

Nelly gives back to the community through his not-for-profit organization 4Sho4Kids Foundation, which serves the African American and minority communities.

$\mathcal{S}$atchel Paige

1905–1982
BASEBALL PLAYER

eroy "Satchel" Paige is said to be one of the greatest and most famous baseball pitchers of all time. Although records are incomplete, Paige often is credited with three hundred career shutouts and fifteen hundred games, which includes countless appearances in exhibition games against all levels of competition in the United States and elsewhere.

His nickname, Satchel, is said to have come from his job carrying bags at the railroad station in Mobile, Alabama, at the age of seven. His pitching style, which included a signature "hesitation" pitch, may have come from his years of throwing rocks at other kids, fooling them into ducking early. Paige learned his control of the ball from the Birmingham Black Baron players, who taught him to throw a Coke bottlecap until he could "nip the frosting off a cake." Paige called that pitch his "be ball," because "it be where I want it to be."

Paige was born in Mobile in 1905 or 1906. (His exact birth date is unknown.) In 1926, he began playing professional ball, and he played for a variety of teams in the Southern and Midwestern states. Paige became known for his hard fastball, his hesitation pitch, and his crowd-pleasing showboating, which included double and triple windups. Because of his power to draw crowds, often he was hired out to teams struggling to stay afloat. Paige went wherever there were job opportunities, playing baseball in Cuba, the Dominican Republic, and Mexico.

In 1939, Paige began a nine-year stint with the Kansas City Monarchs and led them to four consecutive Negro American League pennants and a Negro World Series championship in 1942. Jackie Robinson broke the color barrier in the Major Leagues in 1947, and Paige joined the Cleveland Indians the following year. By then he was forty-two or forty-three, which made him the oldest rookie in history. He posted a 6–1 record to help the team clinch the American League title and proceed to the World Series. Paige went on to play with the St. Louis Browns, where he won twelve games and saved ten. In 1965, at age sixty or older, he pitched three scoreless innings in a special appearance with the Kansas City Athletics.

In 1971, Paige became the first Negro League star inducted into the National Baseball Hall of Fame. He is remembered for one of his so-called rules for staying young: "Don't look back— something might be gaining on you."

Michael Spinks

1956–

Leon Spinks

1953–

PRIZE FIGHTERS

ichael and Leon Spinks, the first brothers to win gold medals in the same sport at an Olympic game and the first to win world professional boxing titles, were born in St. Louis on July 11, 1953, and July 13, 1956, respectively.

Michael became a world heavyweight champion in 1985, when he defeated Larry Holmes in a fifteen-round decision. His road to the top was not as swift as that of his brother. He began his professional career in 1977 and within four years had won the World Boxing Association light heavyweight crown. Michael gained twenty-five pounds and in September of 1985, he became the first reigning light heavyweight champion to defeat a heavyweight champion when he won the International Boxing Federation Heavyweight Title.

He lost the title because he did not make a mandatory defense against a number-one contender. Michael later fought Mike Tyson in 1988, and lost the bout in ninety-one seconds, in the fourth-shortest heavyweight title match in history.

During his career Michael logged thirty-two fights with thirty-

one wins, twenty-one with knockouts, and a single loss. In 1994, he was inducted into the International Boxing Hall of Fame.

Leon came to fame when he defeated Muhammad Ali for the undisputed Heavyweight Championship of the World, one of the biggest upsets in boxing history. Ali later regained the title in a rematch with Leon in a unanimous fifteen-round decision. After the loss to Ali, Leon disappeared from the boxing scene. Earlier in his career, Leon had won a gold medal in the lightweight division at the 1976 Summer Olympic Games in Montreal and the World Amateur Boxing Championships in Havana, Cuba, two years earlier.

During his career as a professional fighter, Leon had an overall record of twenty-six wins, seventeen losses, and three draws, with fourteen knockout wins.

$\mathcal{D}$onald Suggs

1932–

PUBLISHER, ORAL SURGEON, CIVIL RIGHTS ADVOCATE, AND ART PATRON

$\mathcal{D}$onald Suggs, an oral surgeon by profession, is described by many as a Renaissance Man. Except for a three-year stint in the US Armed Forces, Suggs has lived and worked in St. Louis since 1957. He has received many civic awards, including being named the 2004 St. Louis Citizen of the Year.

Active in the civil rights movement of the 1960s and 1970s, Suggs was chairman of the Poor People's March on Washington in 1968. Later, he was founder and chairman of the African American Continuum Theatre Company, organized to bring noncommercial African American artistic endeavors to St. Louis. From 1970 to 1989, he was president of the Alexander-Suggs Gallery of African Art, based in St. Louis and New York City. He also was a founding member of the Center for African Art (now the Museum of African Art in New York City) and was a member of the board of directors of the Studio Museum in Harlem.

In 1981, Suggs was part of a group that bought the nearly bankrupt *St. Louis American* newspaper. He was named publisher in 1984, and since then, the weekly paper has grown from annual revenues of approximately $600,000 and six employees to annual revenues of $3 million and twenty-four employees. Today the paper is Missouri's largest Black-owned newspaper and reaches more

than 45 percent of the St. Louis African American community. For a number of years, the paper has received the National Newspaper Publishers Association's coveted Russwurm Award for excellence in journalism.

Suggs's service on the United Way executive board includes founding the Charmaine Chapman Society and also involvement with the Alexis de Tocqueville Society, both of which encourage African Americans to contribute to the United Way. Suggs was the first African American president of the Convention and Visitors Bureau of St. Louis. He also has served as president of Arch Concessions and has been a partner with D&D Concessions and the City Plaza Project. In 2020, Suggs received the Arch Grants' Entrepreneur Award.

Born in East Chicago, Suggs graduated with BS and DDS degrees from Indiana University. He completed post-graduate work at Washington University and Homer G. Phillips Hospital. He was chief of oral surgery at Dover Air Force Base in Delaware and was the first African American associate clinical professor at Saint Louis University Dental School. Suggs holds honorary doctoral degrees from the University of Missouri–St. Louis, Harris-Stowe University, Saint Louis University, and Washington University in St. Louis.

Clark Terry

1920–2015
Musician and Educator

C lark Terry—an internationally renowned jazz flugelhornist, trumpeter, and educator—developed a love for music at an early age. This passion inspired Terry to create his own music with a piece of garden hose and other discarded items. Over time, his neighbors tired of hearing Terry make sounds on his makeshift contraptions, and they bought him a trumpet for $12.50 at a pawnshop. Terry taught himself to master the instrument.

Born in St. Louis on December 10, 1920, Terry was the seventh of ten children born to May and Clark Terry. He attended Vashon High School and performed in small clubs in St. Louis before he entered the Navy in 1942. While in the Navy, Terry played with the US Naval Band at the Great Lakes Naval Station in Chicago. After his discharge from the service, he joined bands led by the day's headliners: Lionel Hampton, George Hudson, and Count Basie.

Terry's big break came in 1951, when he joined the Duke Ellington Band. As a member, he made good use of the opportunity to be introduced to the "University of Ellingtonia" and also to obtain a reputation for playing a wide range of musical styles and techniques, from swing to hard bop. In 1959, Terry left Ellington to play with Quincy Jones and to work as a freelance studio artist in New York.

In 1960, Terry became the first African American on the payroll

at the National Broadcasting Company after the Urban League confronted NBC about its lack of African American musicians. Terry remained with *The Tonight Show Starring Johnny Carson* for twelve years and was often a featured trumpeter. When the show moved to California, Terry remained in New York, touring the country and performing in Africa, the Middle East, and Pakistan as a goodwill ambassador for the US State Department. Until his death in 2015, Terry continued to tour, perform concerts, and teach young musicians.

During his career, Terry played with almost every accomplished jazz musician, composed more than two hundred jazz songs, received thirteen honorary doctorates, and played for seven US presidents. He received a Grammy Award, two Grammy certificates, three Grammy nominations, a German knighthood, induction into the Jazz Hall of Fame, and the prestigious French Order of Arts and Letters. Terry appeared on 905 known recording sessions, making him the most prolific jazz trumpet player in history.

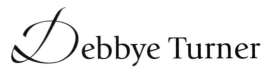

Debbye Turner

1965–

MISS MISSOURI AND MISS AMERICA

A beauty queen, a veterinarian, a television reporter, and a motivational speaker, Debbye Turner loves animals. As a child she would cry whenever she saw an injured or ailing animal. When she was thirteen, she spent the summer observing at the family veterinarian's office, and there she found her calling. In high school, she focused on advanced science courses and participated in civic and leadership clubs, all with the aim of obtaining an academic record that would help her gain acceptance at a veterinary school.

Turner was born in 1965 in Honolulu, Hawaii. Her parents divorced while she was very young. Money was tight, and she worked hard in school in the hope of earning academic scholarships. Turner's life changed after she represented the Future Business Leaders of America in the Jonesboro (Arkansas) High School Valentine Sweetheart Pageant—and won.

One of the judges, a director for one of the Miss America preliminary pageants, asked Turner to enter the Miss Jonesboro Pageant. Turner was not interested until she learned that beauty pageants were the largest source in the world of scholarships for women. Turner realized this might be a way to pay for her education and reach her career goal. After winning the local Miss Jonesboro Pageant, she advanced to the Miss Arkansas Pageant, where she placed in the top ten. She entered the contest again for the next two years, and finished as a runner-up both times.

After seven tries in eleven years, Turner qualified for the Miss America Pageant.

While a student in the School of Veterinary Medicine at the University of Missouri, she woke early every day to prepare for the pageant before heading to classes. Her efforts paid off, and in 1990 Turner was crowned Miss America. She was the third African American winner and the first from Missouri. After a year of service, Turner returned to school and graduated as a doctor of veterinary medicine.

Turner became a spokesperson for the Ralston Purina Company, pursued a career as a veterinarian, and then took a job in television. She was host of *Show Me St. Louis*, a news show on KSDK-TV, and she later worked as a reporter for CBS News. Turner is now a motivational speaker, addressing audiences in the corporate, academic, and community service arenas.

$\mathcal{T}$ina Turner

1939–

SINGER AND ACTRESS

$\mathcal{T}$ina Turner, today one of the world's most popular— and most beautiful—entertainers, was born Anna Mae Bullock on November 26, 1939, in Nutbush, Tennessee. Her parents divorced when she was ten years old. Her mother moved to St. Louis, and her father remarried and moved to Detroit. The Bullock sisters originally went to live with a cousin, but her sister Alline soon moved to St. Louis to be with her mother, and Tina joined them after she turned sixteen.

In St. Louis, Tina enrolled at Sumner High School. The sisters went to clubs in East St. Louis, including Club Manhattan, where her sister's idol, Ike Turner, performed with the Kings of Rhythm. Alline had longed to sing with the group and was promised that one day she would have an opportunity. One evening Alline was asked up on stage. When she refused, Tina started singing. When Ike Turner heard her, he jumped off the stage and asked her to become part of his group.

After several long discussions with her mother, Tina was given permission to sing with Ike. The duo's first hit was "A Fool in Love," which reached No. 27 on the Pop Chart and No. 2 on the R&B Chart. Due to the success of the song, Ike Turner changed the name of the group to the Ike and Tina Revue. The couple married and produced a string of hits, including "River Deep, Mountain High" (1966) and "Proud Mary" (1971), and they gained

widespread recognition and numerous awards. In 1976, because of several instances of domestic violence, Tina left Ike. The couple divorced in 1978 and went their separate ways.

After a slow start, Tina Turner's solo career took off in 1983 with the remake of Al Green's "Let's Stay Together," followed by her much-anticipated solo album, *Private Dancer*, which won four Grammy Awards and sold over 20 million copies worldwide. Her combined album and single sales have been reported to total approximately 180 million copies.

Turner crossed over into Hollywood, appearing in such films as *Mad Max Beyond Thunderdome* starring Mel Gibson, and *The Last Action Hero* with Arnold Schwarzenegger. She also has made several recordings for soundtracks, including "I Don't Need Another Hero," "The Lion King II: Simba's Pride," "Goldeneye," and "He Lives in You."

In 2005, Turner was awarded a Kennedy Center Honor and named as one of Oprah Winfrey's 25 Legendary Black Women. In 2008, *Rolling Stone* named her one of the greatest singers of all time. She has been inducted in the Rock and Roll Hall of Fame, the Hollywood Walk of Fame, and the St. Louis Walk of Fame.

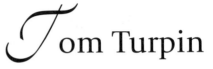

$\mathcal{T}$om Turpin

1871–1922

Songwriter, Musician, and Producer

$\mathcal{T}$homas Milton Turpin is credited as the first African American to publish a rag—"Harlem Rag" in 1897—and the first rag in St. Louis. He was born in Savannah, Georgia, to John L. and Lula Turpin. In the early 1880s, the family moved to St. Louis, where Turpin's father opened a saloon and became active in local politics. Young Turpin and his brother traveled west and invested in the Big Onion Gold Mine, but when they failed to make their fortunes, the brothers returned to St. Louis.

At first, Tom Turpin went to work composing and performing at his father's place, the Silver Dollar, and also at The Castle, operated by Babe Conners. Then, taking a cue from his father, Turpin went into business for himself. First, he opened Turpin's Saloon at 9 Targee Street around 1897, and three years later he opened the legendary Rosebud Café at 2220-22 Market Street.

The Rosebud Café had something for everyone—two bars, a sportsmen's club, gambling facilities, a wine room, and a gentlemen's brothel upstairs. However, Turpin was often the star attraction. He played standing up, with the piano raised to accommodate his three hundred-pound, six-foot frame, so his stomach did not get in the way. In the early years of the twentieth century, the Rosebud Café was the center of the ragtime music world. Turpin gladly accommodated talented musicians, including Scott Joplin. Joplin's composition "Rosebud" was written in 1905 in Turpin's honor.

The 1904 World's Fair in St. Louis, also known as the Louisiana Purchase Exposition, marked the high point for Turpin and his café. After performing on the Pike at the Fair, musicians would move over to the Rosebud and keep the music playing. The establishment even boasted an electric Christmas tree, a true novelty in 1904.

When business slowed down after the Fair, Turpin returned to composing music, which included the "Buffalo Rag" in late 1904. His other compositions included "The Bowery Buck" and "Pan-Am Rag." The Rosebud Café closed in 1906, and Turpin went back to running saloons, dance halls, and sporting houses. He eventually opened the Booker T. Washington Airdome, a vaudeville theatre in a tent-like structure at 2323 Market Street, where he and his brother Charles presented original shows and ragtime-playing competitions. In 1910, Turpin opened the short-lived Eureka Club. Turpin remained in the saloon business and opened another establishment in 1916.

During his later years, Turpin served as a deputy constable in the African American community. He died of peritonitis on August 13, 1922.

Lester Walton

1882–1965

DIPLOMAT AND JOURNALIST

Born in St. Louis in 1882, Lester Walton enjoyed a distinguished career in journalism and diplomacy, though his story is seldom told. After attending public schools and graduating from Sumner High School, in 1902 Walton began his journalism career as a reporter and golf writer for the *St. Louis Star*. He was the first African American to write for a daily paper in St. Louis.

Six years later, Walton left St. Louis for New York, where he became a drama critic and then managing editor of the city's African American newspaper the *New Age*, a position he held until 1914 and again from 1917 to 1919. As a writer, Walton drew attention to stage and screen performers such as Bert Williams and Rosamond Johnson and contributed greatly to their fame. He went on to serve as manager of the Lafayette Theatre and a Black players' company while continuing his journalism career.

Over the years, Walton wrote for the *New York Herald Tribune*, *New York World*, and the *St. Louis Globe-Democrat*. His interest in and knowledge of the African American entertainment world was put to good use during World War I, when he served as a member of the Military Entertainment Service and supervised theatrical productions aimed at African Americans. In the 1950s, Walton became chairman of the Coordinating Council for Negro Performers, which promoted greater integration of African Americans in radio and television.

WALTON IN LIBERIA, PHOTO COURTESY OF NATHAN YOUNG, *YOUR ST. LOUIS AND MINE*

Walton's journalism career enabled him to pursue his international interests. In 1919, he attended the Versailles Peace Conference as a correspondent. In 1933, he visited Liberia and wrote articles for the *New Age* and the *New York Herald Tribune* during a time when relationships among the United States, Great Britain, and Liberian labor and foreign industries were strained. Two years later, President Franklin D. Roosevelt appointed Walton as minister to Liberia, a position he held until 1946. During his tenure as minister, Walton facilitated the negotiation of treaties, including the conditions under which the US government established an army base in Liberia. He also aided in the establishment of Liberia's first international airport and American businesses' interest in rubber production, which was critical for the United States and its allies during World War II.

As a city commissioner, Walton was instrumental in the desegregation of housing in New York, and he worked tirelessly for human rights all his life. Walton retired shortly before he died in 1965 in New York.

$\mathcal{E}$arl Wilson Jr.

1932–2010

FOUNDER, ST. LOUIS GATEWAY CLASSIC SPORTS FOUNDATION

$\mathcal{O}$ut of a desire to elevate the status of African Americans in St. Louis, Earl Wilson Jr., a native of the city, created the St. Louis Gateway Classic Sports Foundation in 1984. Through the foundation, Wilson established and funded full four-year scholarships for African American youth to attend historically Black colleges and universities. Thanks to Wilson, more than $2.6 million was awarded.

Wilson also launched the Gateway Classic Football Game through the foundation in 1997. The annual game between Black college teams is one of the most popular philanthropic events in St. Louis. Wilson also built the Gateway Classic Building, which has been renamed the Earl Wilson Jr. Gateway Classic Building. This $3 million sports facility and community center provides food for thousands of hungry people, toys for children at Christmas, and a Walk of Fame to honor outstanding African American community leaders.

Wilson was born on October 9, 1932. After graduating from Vashon High School, he enrolled in Lincoln University in Jefferson City, Missouri, where he earned a bachelor's degree in education. Years later, he served on the school's board of curators. Wilson attended the US Army Corps of Engineers Officer Candidate School in Port Belvoir, Virginia, and served as a captain. In 1962, he attended the Public Information Officers

School at the US Army North Atlantic Treaty Organization branch in Paris, followed by an enrollment in the IBM European Global Sales School.

Wilson worked for thirty-four years at IBM, during which time he was responsible for a $1.4 billion budget and more than one hundred salespeople. He earned numerous honors at the corporation, including being named IBM Manager of the Year. Wilson retired in 1994 as vice president of marketing. Over the years, Wilson received honorary doctorate degrees from Lincoln, Harris-Stowe State, and Arkansas State universities. In 2000, President Bill Clinton named him to the President's Board of Advisors on Historically Black Colleges and Universities, where he worked to improve student access to higher education.

Wilson died in 2010 after a long illness. In his obituary, Wilson as a youth was described as "scrappy, hard working, a determined boy, the person he would remain as a grown man."

Olly Wilson Jr.

1937–2018
COMPOSER AND MUSICOLOGIST

Olly W. Wilson Jr.—an internationally recognized composer of contemporary classical music, pianist, double bassist, and musicologist—was born in St. Louis in 1937 to Alma Grace Peoples Wilson and Olly Woodrow Wilson Sr. He attended the city's public schools and graduated from Sumner High School, where he played in the school band.

After graduation, Wilson earned a bachelor's degree in music from Washington University in St. Louis, a master's in music from the University of Illinois, and a PhD from the University of Iowa. While living in St. Louis, Wilson played jazz piano with local groups and string bass in several orchestras.

For his work as a composer, Wilson has been recognized by the Guggenheim, Koussevitzky, Rockefeller, Fromm, and Lila Wallace foundations, the National Endowment for the Arts, and the Chamber Music Society of Lincoln Center. In 1968, he received the Dartmouth Arts Council Prize as winner of the first international competition for electronic music for his composition "Cetus." His Guggenheim Fellowship in 1971 allowed him to live in Ghana to study African music and languages, where he later returned as a visiting scholar at the University of Ghana.

Wilson's works have been commissioned and performed by philharmonic orchestras in Boston, Chicago, Moscow, and New York and by symphony orchestras in Detroit, St. Louis, and San

Francisco, as well as by other musical ensembles in the United States and abroad. Wilson also was a Fromm composer in residence at the American Academy in Rome and a senior residence fellow at the Rockefeller Foundation Center in Bellagio, Italy.

In recognition of his outstanding work in composition, in 1995 Wilson was elected to the American Academy of Arts and Letters, where he served as vice president from 2003 to 2006. Wilson has taught at Florida Agricultural and Mechanical University and the Oberlin Conservatory of Music. In 2002, Wilson retired from the University of California at Berkeley, where he began his career in 1970 and served as assistant chancellor for international affairs, chairman of the music department, and distinguished chair of music. At the time of his death Wilson served as professor emeritus of music.

Arthur Cortez Shropshire

1909–1988
EDUCATOR AND SCHOOL SUPERINTENDENT

*S*hropshire was described best by his alma mater, Lincoln University, when presented with the University's Distinguished Service Award, as "an individual who was concerned for people and their problems, both in the classroom and in the greater community."

Shropshire was born in Hunnewell, Missouri, on February 2, 1909. After graduation from Douglass High School in Hannibal, Missouri, he went on to further his education at Lincoln University in Jefferson City, where he earned BS and MA degrees and later a Ph.D. from the University of Nebraska. Shropshire began his career in education as a principal at Langston School in DeSoto, Missouri. Seeing a need for African American students to further their education beyond elementary school, he founded the Douglass Cooperative High School in Festus, Missouri, in 1939. This creative and cooperative project provided the only four-year high school for African American children, involving seven counties between St. Louis, Missouri, and Cape Girardeau. State law did not provide for the high school education of African Americans in sparsely populated areas.

After five years, Shropshire left Festus to accept the position of high school principal of Bartlett High School and Supervisor of Negro Schools in St. Joseph, Missouri. In his quest for a position where he could use his skills, Shropshire left St.

FESTUS MISSOURI COOPERATIVE HIGH SCHOOL, PHOTOS COURTESY
OF JOHN A. WRIGHT SR.

Joseph after seven years for Langston University, to serve as director of education, a position he held for twelve years.

In 1963, Shropshire accepted the most challenging position in his career, superintendent of schools for the Kinloch School District in Kinloch, Missouri. At the time he was the only African American school superintendent in the state of Missouri and one of eleven in the country. Kinloch was an African American school district that was struggling for survival. As superintendent, he was able to obtain over $2,000,000 for the school district. Shropshire retired from the superintendency and his educational career in 1973, leaving a proud legacy.

Shropshire was an active member of his profession. As president of the Missouri Negro Teachers Association (1942–44), Shropshire was instrumental in a lawsuit for the equalization of salaries of African American teachers to that of white teachers in the state. Shropshire also played a major role in the collection and recovery of outstanding tuition ($12,844.00) owed Missouri students attending institutions of higher learning outside of the state. At the time, the state universities were segregated, and Black students were provided tuition to attend school outside the state if the desired education was not available at Black institutions in the state.

$\mathcal{F}$r. Augustus Tolton

1854–1897
PRIEST

$\mathcal{A}$ugustus Tolton was born into slavery in Ralls County, Missouri, on April 1, 1854, to Martha Chisley and Peter Paul Tolton. His parents were married in a Catholic wedding ceremony in St. Peter's Church in Bush Creek. From this marriage, three children were born. Augustus was the middle child and was named after his uncle Augustus. At his baptismal, his owner's wife stood as his godmother.

When the Civil War started, his father joined the war on the Union side and died shortly thereafter, leaving his wife to raise the three children. Records show that Martha took the family across the Mississippi River to Alton, Illinois. The children first were enrolled in the all-Black school in Alton. Martha wanted her children to be raised in the church and tried to get her children enrolled in St. Boniface School, but was denied admission. Through the efforts of Father McGirt, pastor of another parish, she was able to enroll the children in St. Peter's.

The Catholic faith was a major part of Tolton's life. He wanted to be a priest, but no seminary was willing to accept a Black student as a novice. Not to be discouraged, he continued his theological studies with private instructions from two pastors in Quincy, Illinois, and college courses at Quincy College. Finally, with the assistance of Father Bernardino dal Vago, the minister general of the Franciscan friars, he was admitted to Urban College, a seminary in Rome, Italy.

Tolton finished his studies and was ordained to the priesthood in Rome on Easter Sunday in 1886 at the Archbasilica of St. John Lateran. The church decided that Father Augustus Tolton's missionary calling was to the United States to serve the Black community.

Some credit him as being the first Black Catholic priest in America. However, historians dispute this assertion. They claim that distinction goes to three brothers: James Augustine Healy, Francis Patrick Healy, and Sherwood Alexander Healy. These three brothers were of mixed race with very strong Caucasian features and were never recognized as part of the Black population.

Tolton was assigned to Illinois to become the priest of St, Joseph Church in Quincy's Black diocese. He was an immediate success. However, over the years he began to meet some resistance from white Catholics and Protestant Blacks who did not want him to attract people to another denomination. He also ran into opposition from the new dean of the parish, who requested that he turn away white worshipers from his services.

Tolton was reassigned to Chicago, where the archbishop charged him with establishing a parish. Dedicated to his mission, he established St. Monica Church in 1893. Tolton's success with the church quickly earned him national attention within the Catholic hierarchy.

Despite of his success, his letters revealed the loneliness he was feeling and the pressures he was confronted with on a daily basis. Fr. Tolton passed away at the age of 43 on July 9, 1897, from heat exhaustion. He is buried in Quincy, Illinois, near his hometown of Alton.

Chester Himes

1909–1984
AUTHOR

Chester himes created a memorable body of work that vividly captured and satirized the life of Blacks in a racist society. In fact, nearly all of his writings addressed the problems of racism.

Himes was born in Jefferson City, Missouri, on July 29, 1909, to Joseph Sandy Himes and Estelle Bomar Himes, teachers at Lincoln University. As a youngster, he was deeply affected psychologically when he accidentally blinded his brother while playing with fireworks. When they went to the hospital, he was refused treatment by white doctors because of Jim Crow laws. This incident helped shape his attitude about race.

Himes was never able to establish roots as a youngster because his father accepted various teaching positions at many different Black colleges in the south and, finally Cleveland, Ohio.

After graduating from Glenville High School in Cleveland, in 1926, he took on a job as a busboy at Wade Park Hotel, where he fell down an elevator shaft. He was awarded a disability pension of $75 a month. Freed from the worry of making ends meet, he enrolled at Ohio State University. He was soon asked to leave after an altercation at a speakeasy. It was during this period that he entered the shady life. A botched robbery and some forged checks earned him two consecutive suspended sentences. Himes came back before the law, in 1928, when he was sentenced to 20 to 30 years of hard labor at Ohio State Penitentiary for armed

CHESTER B. HIMES

Lawrence P. Jackson

A Biography

robbery. While in prison, Himes began writing, and his works were published in national magazines. After serving seven and a half years, Himes was paroled from prison on August 13, 1938, and married Jean Johnson. During the Depression, Himes took on several jobs with the Works Progress Administration (WPA.) During World War II he moved to California and began screenwriting while producing two novels. In his autobiography, he writes of his job as a screenwriter for Warner Brothers and his termination by Jack L. Warner, who reportedly said he did not want any niggers on his lot.

Himes held out little hope that a Black man could live in a society where whites refuse to accept him as equal. He grew tired of the racist conditions in American and after, he separated from his first wife, Jean, he started a period and began to travel. He self-exiled himself in France and make it his permanent home. While in Paris he met and married his second wife, Lesley Packard, a journalist. After he suffered a stroke in 1959, she quit her job, nursed him back to health, and assisted him as his informal editor, proofreader, and confidante.

Himes flourished in Europe and won honors. His Harlem Detective series of novels, featuring Grave Digger Jones and Coffin Ed Johnson, enjoyed rave reviews in Europe. His most celebrated book in America was *Cotton Comes to Harlem*, which became a movie in 1970.

Later in life, he returned to America to give lectures and do booksignings. He eventually moved to Moraira, Spain, where he died on November 2, 1984.

Brittany Packnett Cunningham

1984–

ACTIVIST, EDUCATOR, AUTHOR

Brittany Packnett Cunningham was named by *Time* magazine in 2015 as one of the "12 New Faces of Black Leadership," named to the *Root* magazine's 100 Most Influential African Americans in 2015 and described as "a bridge over turbulent, troubled waters," and cited by *Ebony* magazine in its 2015 Power 100 list.

Cunnigham was born in St. Louis, Missouri, in 1984. Her father, a pastor and ordained minister in the Baptist Church, is credited with leading her in a commitment for social justice. She earned a bachelor of arts degree in African and American Studies from Washington University in St. Louis. Following graduation, she became a third-grade teacher for Teach for America (TFA) in Washington, D.C., and earned a master's degree in secondary education from American University. While in Washington she served as a legislative assistant to Congressman William Lacy Clay Jr., of Missouri.

After her time on the Hill, Cunningham served on Teach for America's Government Affairs team and volunteered as founding co-chair of the Collective-DC, an organization for TFA alumni of color. She later served as a director of government affairs for TFA. Cunningham was essential in securing greater federal support for TFA. She partnered with Congressman John Lewis for a national

conversation on inspiring more African American men to increase their presence among the nation's teachers. Under Cunningham's leadership as vice president of national community alliances for TFA in 2016, the organization launched its first crusade for civil rights and equality.

From 2012 to 2016, Cunningham led a regional TFA team that served 20,000 St. Louis-area students, creating a strategy to boost student achievement, teacher satisfaction, and diversity. During this time, she became involved in the protest that erupted after a police officer shot and killed an unarmed 18-year-old Black teenager, Michael Brown, in Ferguson, Missouri. Using social media, including Twitter, Cunningham gained recognition as she countered prevailing attitudes and schooled the media on education, voting rights, and equal pay. Because of her involvement, Missouri Governor Jay Nixon appointed Cunningham to the Ferguson Commission he established to respond to the unrest.

In the summer of 2015 Cunningham co-founded Campaign Zero, a policy platform designed to end police violence. That same year she was appointed to President Barack Obama's Task Force on 21st Century Policing, which emerged at the height of the police violence crisis.

Cunningham has traveled extensively in America and abroad, imparting lessons on movement building, social impact, leadership, and intersectional feminism to diverse audiences. Because of her activism, she is a regular contributor to NBC and MSNBC.

About the Authors

*J*ohn A. Wright Sr. is a retired educator who has lived in Missouri all his life. He has served in positions ranging from classroom teacher to superintendent of schools. He has a BA from Harris Teachers College and a ME and PhD from Saint Louis University. He is coauthor of *Extraordinary Black Missourians* and *Ethnic St. Louis*, both by Reedy Press. John is also the author of twelve other books on local and regional history.

*S*ylvia A. Wright is a retired nurse educator who has lived in Missouri most of her life. She holds BSN and MSN degrees from Washington University and a ME from University of Missouri. She is coauthor of *Extraordinary Black Missourians* by Reedy Press and *Carondelet* by Arcadia Press. Sylvia has assisted her husband, John Wright Sr., in writing twelve books and articles on St. Louis and regional history.

ohn Wright Jr. is a proud St. Louisan. Born, raised, and educated in St. Louis, he has worked and lived in St. Louis with his wife and two children. At present, he is a school teacher in the St. Louis Public School District. John has degrees in Advertising, Speech, Curriculum, and Technology, and a doctorate in Educational Leadership. He is a coauthor of *Images of Modern America: African American St. Louis* by Arcadia Press.

$\mathcal{I}$ndex